ZIONISM, LIBERALISM, AND THE FUTURE OF THE JEWISH STATE

Centennial Reflections on Zionist Scholarship
and Controversy

Edited by

Steven J. Zipperstein

and

Ernest S. Frerichs

THE DOROT FOUNDATION
Providence, Rhode Island

Library of Congress Control Number: 00-131801

ISBN 0-9700115-0-4

Printed in the United States of America
by RR Donnelley & Sons, Harrisburg, VA

The Dorot Foundation
439 Benefit Street
Providence, RI 02903
www.dorot.org

CONTENTS

Preface
Ernest S. Frerichs   *v*

Introduction
Steven J. Zipperstein   *1*

Zionism and the Liberal
Imagination
Steven J. Zipperstein   *8*

Individualism and Collectivism
in Zionist Culture and Modern Israel
Yaron Ezrahi   *30*

Zionism and the Arab World
Itamar Rabinovich   *47*

The Zionist Legacy
and the Future of Israel
Shlomo Avineri   *77*

Index of Contributors   *88*

Conference Program   *90*

PREFACE

The Dorot Foundation's sponsorship of the conference, "Truth From the Land of Israel: Reflections on Zionism's Successes, Failures, and Prospects at 100," reflected not only the significance of a centennial, but also a strong interest in Ahad Ha'am by the Foundation's late President, Peter Ungerleider. From early in his life Peter read and reread Ahad Ha'am, distributing freely and frequently copies of Ahad Ha'am's essays to any acquaintance who expressed even minimum interest.

We regret that Peter did not live to be involved in the conference sessions, and we dedicate this publication to Peter's memory. Through the conference and through this publication, the Dorot Foundation is seeking to extend Peter's devotion to Ahad Ha'am, appealing to the circle of those whose vision of Zionism is refracted through the approach of Ahad Ha'am.

Such a conference could not occur without the cooperation of many persons. First, the Foundation wishes to thank publicly Professor Steven J. Zipperstein, Daniel E. Koshland Professor in Jewish Culture and History, Stanford University, whose consultancy enabled us to conceive and effect a conference intellectually appropriate to the intent of the conference.

We were delighted to be joined in our sponsorship of the conference by the New School for Social Research and by the YIVO Institute for Jewish Research. Judith Friedlander, Dean of the Graduate Faculty of Political and Social Science at the

New School, provided a fine setting for our conference in the Swayduck Auditorium of the New School and made her own significant contributions to the quality of the conference discussion.

Included in this publication are the plenary papers presented at the conference. These plenary papers, however, needed a sensitive and informed group of scholars who could convey the relationship of the plenary papers to the conference theme. We are deeply grateful to those scholars who joined us in the conference as panelists, respondents, and panel chairpersons. The conference program includes their names and is printed at the conclusion of this publication.

Finally, this conference would not have occurred without the dedicated efforts of two Dorot Foundation staff members. Jennifer Levine managed very successfully all the graphics and advertising for the conference. Debra Kellstedt was the Conference Coordinator and her involvement and insight contributed decisively to the success of the conference.

The Dorot Foundation expresses publicly our appreciation of the efforts of all these contributors—consultants, co-sponsors, conference participants, and Dorot staff. Together they created a conference that we share with you in part in this publication.

Ernest S. Frerichs
Executive Director, Dorot Foundation

INTRODUCTION

Steven J. Zipperstein

The essays in this volume were originally delivered as lectures at a conference entitled "Truth From the Land of Israel: Reflections on Zionism's Successes, Failures, and Prospects at 100." The title was meant as a grateful nod, an acknowledgment of intellectual debt to the Hebrew essayist, Ahad Ha'am, the penname of Asher Ginsberg (1856-1927).

Ahad Ha'am's provocative, influential series of articles entitled "Truth From the Land of Israel," published in the 1890s, provided intellectuals in the Zionist movement—and also some at its periphery—with the vision of a stringently moral nationalism, empathetic, and capable of satisfying its own people's demands without hurting others (it was hoped), at least not too much. His thinking left a decisive imprint on Gershom Scholem, Judah Magnes, Martin Buber, Mordecai Kaplan, and many others.

Eventually Ahad Ha'am's standing came to be, perhaps, greater outside Israel than inside, where today, when his name is cited, it tends to evoke images of fussiness, of carping: a sort of Jewish Mencken, if you will, without the Baltimore journalist's droll humor. Still, for those who still read him, what remains most vivid about Ahad Ha'am's work is its interplay between love for one's own people and uncompromising self-criticism, a dedication to a nationalist cause, and the obligation to call it to task—mercilessly, and also lovingly—when it stumbles.

The conference, sponsored by the Dorot Foundation and held at the New School for Social Research in October 1998, brought together leading liberal and left-wing intellectuals and scholars from Israel and North America who are inspired, however broadly, by such sentiments. These included Menachem Brinker, Mitchell Cohen, Derek Jonathan Penslar, Leon Wieseltier, Yael Tamir, Judith Friedlander, Tony Judt, Anita Shapira, Adi Ophir, Yael Zerubavel, Michael Walzer, Avishai Margalit, and Fritz Stern, as well as the authors of the essays in this volume. The conference gave them the opportunity to mark the centenary of Zionism as seen through an Ahad Ha'amist lens; hence the subtitle: "Reflections on Zionism's Successes, Failures, and Prospects."

The essays in this volume, examine that interplay between critical appraisal and celebration of Zionism, with an emphasis on what Shlomo Avineri calls in his contribution to this volume the "open wounds" of the Zionist project. The conference took place at a time when the Israeli peace camp, to which nearly all the speakers at the conference feel an affinity, was in disarray, with the Oslo accords, it seemed, all but dead, and with Netanyahu's erratic premiership still uncannily secure. Ehud Barak's victory in the recent Israeli elections raises new hope, which makes the issues discussed here all the more pertinent.

The essays included here are not dispassionate scholarship. They are deeply engaged pieces produced by scholars of Zionism and the Middle East, and they are written from, roughly speaking, a common perspective on things Jewish: on the origins and prospects of the Jewish state, its culture, its politics, and its relations with its Palestinian neighbors. This perspective is one sympathetic to the aspirations of Zionism as a movement that gave the Jewish people a new, vital political life, and it is one that, at the same time, insists that these must be enjoyed always with a keen awareness of when national needs become a collective nightmare. The essays in this volume also ask, pointedly, to what extent a Zionist perspective on things retains its relevance as a way of understanding past and future. Is a "post-Zionist" framework more revealing, more defensible morally, and more illuminating in terms of its historical framework?

Three of the four authors in the volume are Israelis; my essay is the only one written by someone living outside Israel. But the disjuncture, once quite real, between how Israel is seen by its own in contrast to the perspectives of outsiders, has waned much in the last decade, in particular.

Yaron Ezrahi's intriguing essay helps explain why. Ezrahi, a prominent Hebrew University political theorist, argues, much as he does in his superb, widely discussed book, *Rubber Bullets: Power and Conscience in Modern Israel*, that Israel is currently extricating itself from once-dominant collectivist preoccupations and moving closer to societal forms identical, in effect, to those of the West, especially of the United States. Past patterns were the outgrowth of Israel's mostly Russian-Jewish ideological origins, threats to its security, and the task of building a new state out of an exceptionally variegated, large immigrant community. Fifty years later, with Israel now militarily secure and economically stable, this transformation, as Ezrahi sees it, is long overdue.

Ezrahi remains alert to the underbelly of westernization, which could so thoroughly normalize contemporary Israel (as some, indeed, fear) as to render the differences between, say, Tel Aviv and Van Nuys, all but irrelevant. The risk, as he sees it, is real, and it is one that must be confronted directly. He predicts that at the cutting edge of Israeli culture in the near future are once-excoriated features previously denounced as "self-indulgent hedonism, egotistic materialism, and legal formalism." These must be, at least on some level, made a part of how Israelis behave, how they think of themselves, their pleasures, their obligations, and their future. And these patterns, he hopes, will be integrated into Israeli life without the more disintegrative implications of western individualism—its anomie, its "flat individualism." "Like English, French, and American individualism, Israeli individualism must be forged from local materials," he writes.

The building materials of this new, individualistic order remain obscure, of course. He begins his essay with what I suspect is a rather lavish bow in the direction of what he identifies as the more liberal, even secular moments in classical Jewish texts that offer a guide for contemporary Israeli life. "Those who seek support for liberal individualism in Jewish classical texts and Jewish general culture need not despair," he asserts. No doubt, a good many (albeit random) references can be found to support such claims in classical Jewish literature, whose main thrust, however, is not surprisingly inimical to Ezrahi's aspirations of a liberal, individualistic Jewish culture. True, since Zionism originated in the late nineteenth century, its secular supporters have sought to cobble together Jewish cultural foundations no less authentic, no less comprehensive, and no less definitive than were those of its theological precursors. Ahad Ha'am, in fact, was the name most closely associated with such efforts, which, as Ezrahi knows well, have weathered rather poorly in the last century. No liberal ideology can compete on terms similar to those of theology; liberalism implies a conflicted terrain, a degree of relativism, and choice that leaves uncertain, and inevitably so, the Judaic content of Israeli identity in the future.

"To be an Israeli is, at least for secular Israelis, increasingly an act of improvisation, of trying, exploring, experimenting, and moving between several possible spaces and identities. It is hardly conceivable, not even desirable of course, that liberal individualism or its post-modern mutations could ever become a total alternative to Israeli collectivism." Here Ezrahi is, I suspect, closer to the mark. But does this mean the onset of the culture of the shopping mall? Ezrahi's answer would be that this is worth the risk, and also that such new cultural forms will help inspire other essential changes such as new relationships between Israelis and Palestinians. These require, as he sees it, a muting of older, collectivist, ideological motifs, and a highlighting of the preeminence of individuals, their needs, their pleasures, and their aspirations.

What remains in such a society in terms of the distinctiveness of Jewish culture is among the themes addressed by Shlomo Avineri, the distinguished statesman and author of important books on Marx, Hegel, and the Zionist thinkers Hess and Arlosoroff. He is less uncomfortable than Ezrahi with the prospect of an Israeli state still nurtured by Zionism, but, much like Ezrahi, the immediate backdrop to his article is an argument for the forging of an Israeli consensus for a stable peace with Palestinians. He sees this as critical and predicated on "the principle of partition of the historical Land of Israel—the idea of two states for two nations." This requires a major conceptual shift in Israel, one in which older, collectivist principles could well be sacrificed for "an abstract, theoretical secularism." Still, Avineri argues for the prospect of an expansive, culturally rich Jewish state that is, at one and the same time, inimical to all civil discrimination against its minorities, yet discriminates on what he calls "the symbolic level."

What he means is the retention of the Israeli national anthem, the "Hatikva," for example—which, of course, the ultra-Orthodox in Israel, Israel's Arab citizens, and some secular Israelis too feel should now be abandoned. This cultural convention is, he suggests, no more exclusionary than the British "God Save the Queen." And British cultural precedents, Avineri seems to suggest, are not nearly as salient for Israel as the American motifs that so attract Ezrahi. Avineri argues that symbols of Israeli solidarity are likely to be replicated eventually in a future Palestinian state, with cultural fixtures like the "Hatikva" and its Palestinian counterpart coexisting, hopefully in a civil order that guarantees full rights to minorities while sustaining distinctive norms.

Itamar Rabinovich, a prolific, influential historian of the Middle East, and now President of Tel Aviv University, provides an authoritative, lucid portrait of Arab-Israeli relations, with an emphasis, as he puts it, on the impact on the Palestinians, already in the late '30s, of their loss of "control over the course of events." This was the product of more than merely the ability of Jews to better navigate the larger political terrain. No less important was the early, emphatic unwillingness of Palestinians to tolerate any politicized Jewish presence in the region of ancient Israel, and the indifference to the Palestinians shown for so long by so much of the Arab world. Rabinovich's essay provides an essential, chronological framework for understanding the perilously long road to Oslo and beyond. Oslo remains, as Rabinovich argues, an invariably flawed but still-feasible framework for peace.

In the last decade in particular, as both Rabinovich and I argue, much of our historical understanding of what Zionism has wrought has been expanded without the self-censorship and defensiveness of the recent past. There now exists an often deeply unsettling but also striking similarity between at least some Israeli and Palestinian versions of their respective historical experiences in the last century. The essays in this volume are all written in the wake of these new historiographical and political developments; they are written, it is fair to say, with love and also unease. They are exercises in scholarship and politics, efforts at celebration and also at a sober, honest reckoning with a past. They insist on facing the grimmer moments of this past without losing perspective on its triumphs which, of course, remain, as they must, tales of defeat for another people. These are essays that seek to subvert the telling of Zionism as either good or bad, that undermine the telling of it in simple nationalist or "post-Zionist" terms—the one, increasingly, a mirror-image of the other—and they point toward a fuller, more humane sense of history and its implications.

ZIONISM AND
THE LIBERAL IMAGINATION

Steven J. Zipperstein

In an article published soon after the end of the Six Day War, the Israeli journalist Amos Elon told of listening together with a tank regiment south of Beersheva to the disastrous, meandering speech of Prime Minister Levi Eshkol in late May of 1967, his infamous "stammering speech." In a broadcast meant to reassure his people, the elderly, amiable Eshkol was widely perceived as having been so stricken by fear by the prospect of a new war with the Arabs that he was unable to talk. If anything, the radio address exacerbated the mounting tension of the weeks prior to the outbreak of the war. Elon writes that as soon as the speech ended, an officer sitting near him muttered, "Our real problem is not Nasser, but the Second Aliyah."[1]

Eshkol was a leading member of the generation of the Second Aliyah—the turn-of-the-century Jewish pioneers, mostly from the Russian empire—who left their definitive imprint on the making of the Israeli state. This generation came of age at much the same time as that of Ramsay MacDonald. Yet long after MacDonald or, for that matter, Winston Churchill abandoned center stage, these uncannily resilient socialists from Plonsk or Poltava remained at the helm of Israeli politics, the kibbutz movement, the Histadrut Labor Federation, and the array of interlinking institutions built on what a good many of them continued to insist were underpopulated, feudal lands.

One such pioneer is sketched, soon after his death, in Yaakov Shabtai's brilliant novel of the late seventies, *Zikhron Devarim, Past Continuous*. The narrator, the unhappy, aimless son of one of these indominable men, provides what seems at first a believable if also decidedly unattractive description of his father. Soon, the depiction is rendered so dark, so mendacious, so impossible to believe that it is obvious that Shabtai means for us to understand that it can't be taken at face value—although at the same time, we're left to assume that it captures something of the truth. This deceased pioneer of Israel was, as the narrator tells us,

> a Zionist and a Socialist [who] believed in plain living, hard work, morality, and progress...and hated right-wing nationalists, people who got rich or wasted money on luxuries, and people who told lies about the Land of Israel, and all this as part of a system of clear, fixed, uncompromising principles embracing every area of life.... He knew what was right and good, not only for himself but for others, and could not tolerate error or sin...because his integrity verged on insanity and his sense of justice was dark and murky, and above all because he had a tyrannical, uncontrollable desire to impose his principles on the whole world....[2]

"Our real problem is not Nasser, but the Second Aliyah." Nasser's army was prepared, or so it was then feared, to do away with Israel; what comparable aggression could the few thousand ideologically preoccupied youth of the Second Aliyah have committed? Yet this judgment of Zionism's pioneers, sardonic to be sure, has more so than ever before a contemporary ring to it. In the intervening years, the Egyptian border has been made into the site of a cool but reasonably secure peace, but no comparable peace reigns today in the depictions of the Second Aliyah or its impact on Zionism.

This essay seeks to capture a changing sense among some

Israelis and American Jews, and others too, about this past, its achievements, its failures, and a changing sense of what transpired in history that may in turn contribute to a different understanding of what Israel might be in the future. Quite intentionally, I collapse distinctions between liberalism and the left, at least insofar as these political forces exist in contemporary Israeli life: As important as such distinctions once were, little remains of the Israeli left except what would elsewhere be called liberalism. Labor Zionism built the state; the first professionally trained, still justly influential Israeli generation of historians of Jewish Palestine (Anita Shapira, Israel Kolatt, Yosef Gorni) have written mostly about Labor Zionism; but they're, in effect, in-house critics.[3] Much of the existing scholarship on the history of Zionism, including my own, has until recently been produced by such sympathizers. This now is changing, and impact of this new work—often flawed, and at the same time, often important—is still being registered.

The ensuing debate constitutes more than an academic debate. Or rather it is an academic debate with broad cultural ramifications beyond the walls of the academy. At its core, it is a dispute about the central assumptions of Zionism. And this new work has played some small role, it seems to me, in haunting the centenary of Zionism—in casting an often unarticulated but palpable discomfort over attempts to mark the event. This essay seeks to take measure of this scholarship, and also to indicate how it might better be integrated into the larger body of historical literature on the emergence of the Israeli state. In short, I seek here to demystify both the more standard scholarship on Zionism as well as revisionist work on the subject.

It has long been recognized that a mostly incomprehensible distance has separated the grand masters of Zionist ideology—say, Theodor Herzl or Odessa's Ahad Ha'am—from the daily life of the Jewish state. Their bourgeois liberalism never quite caught on (beyond the German Jews, that is, who themselves weren't much influenced by the liberal theorists and who had, at any rate, little impact on the politics of Israel); their teachings often sounded rarefied, even pompous to the more coarsened products of this pioneering milieu. On the whole, the classics of Zionist thought have met with a fate comparable to and probably a good deal worse than that of Ralph Waldo Emerson or Oliver Wendell Holmes in the United States. The prominence granted them in Israeli schools made them not infrequently (in contrast to Emerson) objects of derision rather than simple indifference.

Zionist ideology also came to suffer as something of a victim of its own success: It had sought, beginning in the late nineteenth century, to recover for Jews a sustained political life in the Land of Israel; it had hoped, much like other nationalist movements of East European origin, to produce an authentic and also modern culture. By the late sixties, this ideology was credited with extraordinary success, with little less than with having set in motion a state whose size, military power, and economic and cultural achievements far exceeded the aspirations of all but a handful of its greediest founders.

If Herzl remained a distant, fussy emblem, Ben Gurion and the generation of the Second Aliyah were, by contrast, all too familiar—their presence on the national scene so prolonged, their influence too intrusive (or inspiring) to ignore. This continued long after they formally relinquished political office: Who can doubt that Ben Gurion, sitting in the desert in his book-lined study at Sde Boker—his hands caressing Plato, his wife, Paula, intercepting guests in the next room— wasn't awaiting that call to come back and run things again? This leadership cadre so haunted the next generation and beyond that Yaron Ezrahi's new book, *Rubber Bullets*, makes an eloquent, moving case for little less than a cultural exorcism to relieve today's Israelis from the still-stifling impact, particularly the collectivist ethos. Only then, argues Ezrahi, will Israelis breathe freely; only then will they consume comfortably (although they seem to have learned this particular lesson rather well already), and only then, thinking about individual happiness rather than nationalist aspirations, will they make peace with their neighbors.[4]

It was Ben Gurion who served for as long as anyone could remember as the blunt philosopher-king of Jewish rebirth—the leader most readily associated with the grit and grandeur of this small, beleaguered, then widely admired land. Already in the sixties, much of Israeli politics revolved around reactions—often bitter domestic reactions—to him and his policies. So not surprisingly, much of the more recent scholarship on the making of Israel has concentrated, in one way or another, on Ben Gurion. This drastic alteration in his historical standing represents something of a litmus test for the larger, current reassessment within Israel, and elsewhere in the Jewish world, of the Zionist legacy.

The reassessment of Ben Gurion has arguably proved to be more thoroughgoing than those undergone by any democratic leader of the last half century. Lyndon Johnson, Harry Truman, and even Neville Chamberlain have regained standing over the years. In contrast, Ben Gurion's reputation—despite the prodigious work of his biographer, Shabtai Teveth—is now akin to that of Mitterand: the fate of a political giant who stayed around too long, who attached himself too vigorously to claims of utter integrity, and who refused, until it was too late, to admit error. Both fell hard and fast. To be sure, Mitterand's sins are (by his own admission) clear-cut; Ben Gurion's remain contested, but nonetheless he is badly tarnished.[5]

"I have," writes Amos Oz in 1990, in an essay already dated in its unambiguous admiration, "a very deep-seated attachment to the early Zionist socialists, and my intellectual and emotional views are rooted in their ideology."[6] Oz refers here not to Ben Gurion but to the Tolstoyan Jewish ideologue A. D. Gordon, and the brilliant, tragic Labor Party leader Pinhas Lavon. Still, such declamations now seem truly passé in Oz's own progressive circles, and his more recent statements on this score have in fact taken on a rather more defensive tone. He can't be unaware of how out-of-kilter his stalwart socialist Zionism is in the same circles that so recently celebrated him.

A vivid indication of this current sour mood may be seen in what might seem an unlikely source: a huge, scholarly, and also grimly passionate biography, *Moshe Sharett: Biography of a Political Moderate*, published two years ago by Oxford University's Clarendon Press and written by Hebrew University political scientist Gabriel Sheffer.[7] Here we see, at one and the same time, the savaging of Ben Gurion and a sustained, exhaustive attempt at resurrecting what was, according to this book, the liberal, decent, otherwise marginalized side to the Second Aliyah. The author is acutely (indeed, perhaps even excessively) aware of the furious denials—by "post-Zionists" and others—that this is feasible and that there exists any real difference between the diplomatic tradition of Sharett and the activism of Ben Gurion. At the book's margins, one hears echoes of the many Israeli arguments that preceded Oslo, disputes pitting those favoring military solutions to the confrontation between Jews and Arabs in the Land of Israel against others who have, for the last half century and more, promoted solutions more in keeping with the moderate, donnish, (and in Sheffer's view) prescient Sharett.

Sharett was, for a long time, Ben Gurion's Foreign Minister (and, briefly, Israel's Prime Minister). He was the architect of the Israeli diplomatic corps that for so long played a backseat role to the military in the shaping of political policy, first in Jewish Palestine and then in Israel. His biographer offers, in this the first, comprehensive portrait of Sharett's life, an argument for the superiority of an Israel guided by his spirit, and also, in effect, that of Oslo. In line with the earnest, political ramifications of this message, the author works hard—no doubt, too hard—to shore up Sharett's reputation: He can't resist hounding his nemesis, Ben Gurion. He hurls insults at him, and he can't stop short from calling him truly dreadful names. So unrestrained is the book that Benny Morris, no fan of Israel's first Prime Minister, in a review in *The Journal of Palestine Studies*, takes the author to task for its excessive use of synonyms for evil in its depiction of Ben Gurion. These include "manipulative," "devious," "envious," "deceitful," "hypocritical," "foxy," "aggressive," and "Machiavellian." There are more, too. Morris writes: "Ben Gurion probably was everything that Sheffer says and more. However, the barrage of epithets gradually erodes the author's credibility, driving the nail home and clear through the floor into the neighbor's living room."[8]

This book's unrestrained, unselfconscious fury (it is some 1,100 pages in length, a huge, vengeful, lawyerlike document) is itself the product of Sheffer's continued attachment to Labor Zionism—in the mold of Sharett, that is. It is because Sheffer has not severed himself from Labor's stable that he remains livid—not bemused, contemptuous, or merely sarcastic—when confronting Labor Zionism's singular contribution to Israel's political quagmire since the Six Day War, its mostly dreadful record in Arab-Jewish relations, and its insistence on seeing diplomatic solutions mainly through military eyes. The difference between the moderation of Sharett and the activism of Ben Gurion is, as Sheffer insists, not merely one of style but also of substance—or, more precisely, Sharett's moderation represents an alternative style that, had it been given a chance, could well have had substantive political implications. Stoking Sheffer's rage is the belief that had Sharett been at Israel's helm, he would have avoided the Sinai campaign (he finally, belatedly, broke with Ben Gurion over this campaign). He wouldn't have (Sheffer believes) held onto the lands acquired in the 1967 war, and he would have been better positioned to understand the words of Arab leaders, the pain of Palestinians, and the more noble inclinations of his own people.

Sheffer's insistence on the preeminence of this Zionism with a human face pits him, if you will, not only against the activist legacy of Ben Gurion, but also no less decisively against those to his left who deny that Zionism could ever have been truly moderate, especially in its attitude toward the Arabs. Some twenty years ago, when Shabtai wrote his novel *Past Continuous*, the term Zionist would have been associated in all but the most marginal Israeli circles with, at worst, hollow sentiment, as a byword for nonsense. Now it has taken on (and in much the same milieu) a sometimes far more sinister cast: It belongs in the minds of many to the Jewish messianists of Judea and Samaria, and Israelis have come to assume, whether glumly or admiringly, that the right-wing claim to be the true heirs of Ben Gurion is accurate—that West Bank Ofra, no less than Degania, represents the culmination of the activism of the Second Aliyah.

So it may be said that the unwieldiness of Sheffer's book is itself a sign of the times—a product of its various, overlapping, never-reconciled tasks and its tensions. It is, in this respect, something of a metaphor for the dilemma of the Liberal Zionist tradition that it so breathlessly champions. Not all ungainly books, to be sure, are a sign of confounding times; but this one helps us better appreciate our current dilemma. It is something like looking at oneself in the mirror after a particularly difficult, sleepless night—you're there, but then not entirely. We look at the mirror, a few short years after Oslo, in the midst of what seems a slow, terrible death-dance with the Palestinians, and the strained romanticism, the outdated sense of goodwill, and the desperation of Sheffer's view of past and future all seem painfully reminiscent of our own sometimes more facile assumptions, too.

It is against this backdrop—grim and uncertain, with the Oslo accords already a distant, surreal memory—that the centenary of the Zionist movement (launched in 1897) has been marked. To many of us it remains unclear how this ought best be done. An example of the difficulty liberal Jews have experienced in capturing this anniversary may be seen in the recent issue devoted to the anniversary of Zionism in *Tikkun* magazine (March/April 1998), a periodical that has, of course, long been a resolute voice in support of the Israeli peace camp associated with Amos Oz.

Yet the magazine's issue on Zionism seems, on the surface at least, to put something else in the foreground; the magazine's editor, Michael Lerner, sets the tone with his own lead article entitled "Post-Zionism." What is most striking about this essay is, in fact, its utter conventionality—there is nothing, beyond an odd phrase or two, that is post-Zionist about it. It is essentially standard, liberal/left Zionism, but, as Lerner seems to appreciate, the title remains important in its progressive merchandizing. The title is *Tikkun*'s way of signaling that the piece is really cool, that it embodies just the right stance and at just the right moment. Post-Zionism is a marketing device here, and in this respect, the gesture is little different from, say, Ben and Jerry's choice to name its ice cream after Jerry Garcia, not Wayne Newton.

It is *Tikkun*'s sense of the marketability of post-Zionism, then, that is revealing. Its editor seems intent on underlining that the only truly relevant way to mark the anniversary of Zionism is to insist upon the movement's obsolescence. So, each in its own way, both Sheffer's book (with its relentless desire to salvage the reputation of what it asserts as true Zionism) as well as *Tikkun* (with its eye fixed on the progressive bottom line) demonstrate the difficulty of speaking coherently today about the Zionist past. Increasingly, such talk tends to veer, in Israel and elsewhere, between wild extremes: between defensiveness and sometimes truly astonishing accusations, between old, stale, knee-jerk declamations and charges of sinister Zionist prescience, not excluding charges of little less than a comprehensive plan (dating back to the early 1920s or earlier) to dislodge Palestinians, and of contingency transmuted into clear-cut, bald teleology.

Under the rubric of Post-Zionism are the writings of a rather broad group of historians, sociologists, and philosophers that draws its inspiration, much like that of the work of the so-called new historians, from newly accessible Israeli governmental archives, opened in the 1980s. These have provided sometimes startling data on the origins of the state in 1947/48, its military capacity, and its treatment of Arabs, among other topics.

Those calling themselves new historians, such as Benny Morris, claim for themselves a standing as historical positivists, as dispassionate scholars beyond the fray, unsullied by the partisanship that mars the work of others. Scholars willing to acknowledge themselves as post-Zionist admit that underlying their work are fundamental criticisms regarding the objectives of the Zionist enterprise—not excluding the most basic of all, Jewish sovereignty. Some, such as intellectual historian Amnon Raz-Krakotzkin, political journalist Meron Benveniste, and sociologist Gershon Shaffir, as well as others in Israel, Great Britain, and the United States, have in one way or another sought to revive, after many years of apparent irrelevance, something of the ethos, even the politics of binationalism. Others, such as Ilan Pappe, Joel Beinin, and Zachary Lockman, are closer to an anti-Zionist, Marxist political tradition. What these works share, despite their differences, is a desire to query the wisdom, the cost, and the morality of Jewish nationalism in a land where the success of one nation was bound to signal failure, even tragedy for the other. Here (as in the scholarship of Morris) the ability of Jewish nationalism to navigate between humane, progressive rhetoric and sometimes brutal political and military policy, its pragmatism (which post-Zionism often tends to see as caginess or worse), its lack of empathy regarding Arabs whose desires just didn't matter much among most Zionists on the right or the left, these are among the historical—and all-too-contemporary—issues given prominence.[9]

Here the presumptions of self-avowed, moderate Zionists like Sharett or Berl Katznelson are savaged, often with considerably more vigor than are those of their opponents on the right, whose open belligerency tends almost to be admired for its candor, for a brazenness not unlike that of the scholarly revisionists themselves. No one wedded to a nationalist agenda could have—it is often argued in these circles—substantively improved on Ben Gurion's record; hence, the sins of the fathers are deemed not idiosyncratic but intrinsic.

At its worst, post-Zionism is characterized by the all-too-familiar excesses of moralists: a frigid, narrow haughtiness, and by a lack of empathy for the burdens shouldered by those with whom it refuses to sympathize—in this instance, the builders of the Israeli state. At its best, however, this scholarship compels us to look beyond the edges of the standard accounts of Zionism to see others, Arabs as well as well as many different sorts of Jews, standing there still surprisingly unexamined: a vast, fascinating, sometimes unsettling terrain whose integration into the history of Zionism promises a fuller portrait of Jewish and Arab nationalism, of the lands of Israel, Palestine, and their vicissitudes. This scholarship renders less clear, and usefully so, the lines between revival and colonization, self-reliance and ethnic exclusion, national pride and naked, unrestrained hubris.

It may appear ironic, but it is also appropriate, I think, that this new, intense, sometimes bitter preoccupation with the Zionist past has coincided, more or less, with the Oslo accords, with their call for little less than collective amnesia, for a muting of differences between the national narratives of Palestinians and Jews. "We arrived at an understanding," writes the Foreign Ministry's Uri Savir about his first meeting in Oslo with the Palestinian negotiators. "Never again would we argue about the past.... Discussing the future would mean reconciling two rights, not redressing ancient wrongs."[10] Oslo, like all attempts to reconcile national disagreements, would have been inconceivable without the promise of much lavish forgetting: the willingness of Palestinians to forget past abuse; the ability of Israelis to forget old, sometimes chilling threats as well as terrorism; and the decision of Palestinian nationalists to put aside dreams of a great uprising and its promise to restore all their former lands.

The coexistence of this call for forgetfulness with a heightened, potentially fuller role for history isn't quite as irreconcilable as it may first seem. Above all, what the Palestinians have agreed at least officially to forget is what they had always insisted upon seeing as Zionism's original sin: the Jewish settlement of Palestine and the creation of a Jewish state. Now that such matters—and the various, conflicting details underpinning them—no longer belong, at least to the extent they once did, to the domain of politics, they can be more usefully discussed in a less explosive sphere in which their airing no longer bears the political risks of the recent past. In this regard, Derek Jonathan Penslar has compared the rhetoric of contemporary, revisionist Israeli historiography to the scholarship in the United States in the 1960s reevaluating the origins of the Cold War. This work, too, was often severely moralist; in retrospect, much of it now seems flawed in its marshalling of history to answer questions about the making of the politics of the Vietnam war. Still, in its sweep, its self-aware unorthodoxy, and its belligerency, it helped decisively to clear the air.[11]

As an intensely ideological society, Israel was built on a welter of myths—of origin, of teleology, of morality, and of heroism. It is now time to step back to reassess all these assumptions, their historicity, the relationship between what we would like to believe about ourselves and our people and what transpired. In the end, we're certain to possess a less epic-like tale; but then, who hasn't come in the late twentieth century to distrust—indeed, to deplore—epochal explanations for collective behavior?

It is against this complex, fractured backdrop that the anniversary of Zionism must be marked. How to mark—and also celebrate—the resonance of this movement in such a way that captures with accuracy what it has done for Jews and also what it has done to others?

I'm reminded of Irving Howe, who in an essay of the mid-1950s, "The Age of Conformity," explored the difficulty faced by intellectuals searching for the appropriate language with which to speak critically—but also realistically—about their world, without either mindless sloganeering or undue obsequiousness. He was then describing the middle ground between conformism and visceral radicalism in American society. "Between the willfulness of those who see only terror and the indifference of those who see only health," there is, as Howe insists, the need for truth.[12]

Howe provides a model not only because of his proverbial wisdom, but also because of the paucity of literature in recent years in the United States (or even elsewhere in the western world) that captures the relationship that a liberal or, for that matter, a left-wing Jew might have with the Jewish nationalist enterprise. (Here I shift gears, briefly, from images of Zionism in contemporary Israeli culture to images of Israel in the American Jewish imagination.) A few decades ago, there seemed to be a good many writers who produced serious, sustained work along these lines: for example, Maurice Samuel, Mordecai Kaplan, Chaim Greenberg, Marie Syrkin, Saul Bellow, and Ben Halpern; in France, Albert Memmi and Georges Friedmann; in England, Arthur Koestler. Today, except for the liberal reportage on Israel by Arthur Hertzberg and the essays of Mitchell Cohen, Leon Wieseltier, and Michael Walzer (whose remarkable ruminations on wars, just and unjust, on tribalism, and on so many other features of modern life seem shaped so indelibly by his Zionist preoccupations), one finds little of this.[13]

There is, you may say, something strained, even vaguely pathetic about a Zionist abroad. The jokes about such folk are legion: about their moral surrogacy, the vacuity of their philanthropic Judaism, the hysteria in what they insist on calling politics. Zionist youth movements in the United States have, more or less, closed shop; calls for aliyah in this country are comparable in their likely efficacy (beyond the Orthodox, that is) to calls for a female Orthodox rabbinate; and serious books on Zionism are remaindered fast. I speak from experience.

Yet in Jewish life, few ideas have occupied in this century quite the influence that Zionism has, especially in its liberal or left-wing forms. One looks in vain in recent years, however, for evidence of its wider intellectual impact. To illustrate just this gap, look at the most memorable and most vivid recent treatments of Israeli society produced by North American Jewish intellectuals: It seems to me that these are Ruth Wisse's collection of essays, *If I Am Not For Myself…: The Liberal Betrayal of the Jews*, and Philip Roth's novels, *The Counterlife* and *Operation Shylock*.[14] Coupling Wisse and Roth might appear counterintuitive; I do so to underline the fact that neither draws any inspiration at all from liberal or left-wing Zionism, except, that is, as a foil.

Clearly, there can be no dispute in this regard about Wisse's book, a severe rejection of liberalism and, as she sees it, its crippling legacy. But Roth too makes a no less emphatic, not uncompelling, and, of course, repetitive case in his novels as well as his essays for how Jewishness is for him tribal, local, intimate, and, despite all its erudite talk, essentially uncerebral. It is, as Roth sees it, simply beside the point to view in ideological terms something so messy, so undefinable, and so essentially oral as the experience of living as a Jew. Zionism, perhaps, isn't more absurd than other attempts; indeed, the notion of a Philip Roth preoccupied with any Jewish ideology—whether Zionist or Territorialist—is the one big joke of his *Operation Shylock.*

Whatever one might think their conclusions, both Wisse and Roth look with seriousness and great intelligence at a real, concrete, troubled Israel. More typical, however, in America today are descriptions that see this land as something akin to an unfettered religious theme park, a sort of Mediterranean Celtic ruin. Some such work is quite impressive—for example, Tova Reich's *The Jewish War.*[15] But this is much the same terrain one encounters, with far less success, it seems to me, in Robert Stone's new, unaccountably acclaimed novel *Damascus Gate,* with its modern-day, ersatz Sabbatai Sevi, with his Nathan of Gaza, with these two wild and crazy guys taking to the road in a state of numb incomprehension and in what is meant, I suppose, to serve as contemporary analogues to the trips, real and imagined, of Melville or Blake. The book is intended to be an ecstatic, confounding, verbose tour to the world's monotheistic hot spot; in fact, its many druggy conversations sound much like the sort of thing one overhears in line, late at night, at Tower Records.[16]

How different are Stone's suburban Rasputins from the women and men recorded, in the early 1970s, by that now-forgotten, talented American-Jewish writer, Hugh Nissenson. His *Notes From the Frontier* was written, as were so many books on Israel until the 1980s, from the vantage point of the kibbutz, that "experiment that did not fail" and that continued to serve for Western Jews for so long as the quintessential scene of Israeli life. So when in Nissenson's travelogue, a learned, humane kibbutznik with whom the author talks seeks to define Zionism, the monologue is, quite literally, studded with references to the poet Hayyim Nahman Bialik and other liberal, secular Jewish icons. He provides the following definition for the movement: "Men ... decided to take their fate into their own hands, as if God had never existed. That's what Zionism is, you see. A metaphysical revolt."[17] Nothing would be more alien to recent American portraits of the Jewish state.

Nissenson's portrait is so full of hope, so full of love, and admittedly also laced with denial (Arabs here are nearly always aggressors, and their desires are mysterious and essentially sinister). This is an inspired, heartfelt, and somewhat opaque Jewish liberal manifesto with its foregrounding of egalitarian pioneers and its celebration of secular Jewish commitments. It is also devoid of the many hard, uncomfortable questions about war and peace that would, I suspect, have risen to the surface had it been written only a few years later, after the election of Menachem Begin, the peace with Egypt, and the rise of the Israeli peace movement. "Never such innocence again."

What Zionism wrought, above all, was Jewish sovereignty. Its most singular insight was its insistence that Jewish statelessness could be perilous, even disastrous. Clearly it didn't (and couldn't) foresee the horrors of Nazism, and the leaders of Jewish Palestine responded to Hitler's extermination of the Jews of Europe with much the same confoundment as did Jews elsewhere outside the Nazi net. But to the extent to which any modern Jewish ideology offered insight into the European diaspora and its possible fate—this was Zionism.

Power can corrupt; powerlessness can devastate. Tom Nairn writes in a recent review of a book on Europe's postwar Gypsies, included in his book *Faces of Nationalism*, that "the Roman population has become such a renewed scapegoat because it has no such protection, of any equivalent, for the Zionism which served to rally and direct the identity of the other transnational population once so prominent in Central and Eastern Europe."[18] His claims regarding the popularity of prewar Zionism are no doubt exaggerated, but what interests me here is his juxtaposition of Gypsies and Jews, which is, at first glance, truly jarring. How can one compare a rootless, landless, beleaguered, vaguely threatening, roundly misunderstood population of transients with the Jewish people? How, indeed? Nairn, a good student of modern Europe, appreciates that little more than fifty years ago, this comparison had the most chilling pertinence. That it is no longer apt—and now, indeed, seems almost eccentric—is, as he notes, an achievement of Zionism; Nairn has little sympathy for the movement, but he can't deny it this singular accomplishment.

There is to nationalism a truth that often is, as Nairn has said so pointedly, "non-logical, untidy, refractory, disintegrative, [and] particularistic."[19] It is, if you will, much as Albert Camus said in defense of his refusal to take sides on the Algerian conflict: "I have always condemned terror. Therefore I must condemn a terrorism operating blindly on the streets of Algiers, for example, which one day might strike at my mother or my family. I believe in defending justice, but first I will defend my mother."[20] At the core of all nationalism is the reality—or at least the prospect—of solidarity that, as Yael Tamir has characterized it in her important monograph, *Liberal Nationalism*, offers up, as an ideal, living side by side with those with whom one shares one's most immediate cultural assumptions. This is not, she insists, inconsistent with liberalism and its emphasis on choice, on reflection, and on autonomy. At the center of her argument is an attempt to reconfigure a political universe in which, as she puts it, "nationalists can appreciate the value of personal autonomy and individual rights and freedoms, as well as sustain a commitment for social justice both between and within nations."[21]

In the wake of Oslo, these and similar sentiments began to be translated—laboriously, and, perhaps, in the end, also abortively—into policy. Oslo, for all its many, many shortcomings, is something of a flawed but not uninspiring late-twentieth-century morality tale. Here a medley of middle-aged Palestinians and Israelis, men who attacked together heavy, Norwegian breakfasts, men who shared few illusions, men aware that they were just moments passed their prime—much the same cast of crusty, not unsentimental characters we know well from the Cold War novels of Le Carré—these men were sent by their leaders, who were all in their sixties or seventies, to make peace between inveterate enemies. Not all they did, of course, was pure of motive; not all they did was feasible, or, for that matter, good. They attempted, as such people do, to take advantage of one another; the Israelis, always in Oslo and later too with the upper hand, won most of the rounds.

Still, speaking with one another—at least in better moments—as people worthy of regard and as people worthy of a land of their own, they sat down to talk, at least tentatively, about water and electricity, policing and border controls—the stuff that now and in the future must remain at the center of the more intelligent, relevant talk about Israel and Palestine. Such talk will almost certainly have, in the near future, a greater impact on writing about Israel than on its politics. Still, in its foregrounding of social, political, and economic reality—neither rarefied sentiments nor rejectionism but rather the everyday grind of living side by side in the Middle East—Oslo established a consensual, middle-of-the-road benchmark for how this region and its problems might be better understood far beyond the writing desk.

"There are more versions of what happened in our Valley than there are people it happened to,"[22] says a character in Meir Shalev's anti-epic, the remarkable novel of the making of Jewish Palestine, *The Blue Mountain*, or *Roman Russi*. It's time to hear them all. Many, like myself, will call ours Zionist; others will not. We'll argue about the various conflicting versions; about past hurts, politics, guilt, the responsibilities one feels to one's own people, and the limit to such responsibilities. Some of what will be said will be furious or defensive; some of it will sound much like the forlorn letters of a lover spurned, something like Yaakov Shabtai's angry, obsessive child, albeit some twenty years older. We'll argue then about precisely the sorts of the things that the Oslo negotiators knew had to be avoided there. And we'll seek to write honestly about the history of water and electricity, about roads, and about ideas that inspired and, at times, also turned sour.

Many of us will mark this history as a crucial moment in our people's history, while recognizing that clearly, the achievements of this movement fell short of the redemption it promised. Even its most severe critics would be hard pressed to claim that it failed as badly as did most other ideas in this century that promised a secular redemption. No doubt, much like Sharett's recent biographer, there will be those who will insist that the better face of Zionism has yet to be seen—or, for that matter, was seen, however fleetingly, in Rabin's own, strange, personal odyssey, a political evolution itself almost too richly emblematic. What I mean by this is his belated recognition in the last months of his life that diplomacy and not militarism—that the decent, honorable treatment of one's neighbors and not their glum submission—was the best, the most practicable, and the most lasting route to a good future for Jews and Arabs in those lands that both so treasure. Wolves have lain down with wolves: They've broken bread; they've proven that they can begin, at least, to break old, wretched patterns. This happened just a few, short years ago, and although it now sometimes seems like a chapter in an old, forlorn textbook, may the memory of its better moments remain a blessing.

Notes

*I wish to express my gratitude to my Stanford colleagues, Aron Rodrigue and Joel Beinin, with whom I spoke often about this text. I'm also grateful for the advice of Mitchell Cohen, Martin Jay, Tony Judt, Eli Shaltiel, Anita Shapira, and Derek Jonathan Penslar. I thank my research assistant, Jim Finstein, for his ingenuity and good humor. I also thank the wonderful staff at the Dorot Foundation, in particular, its Executive Director Ernest Frerichs, and his associate Debra Kellstedt for their excellent work on the conference held at the New School for Social Research where this was first delivered as a keynote address. I gave a version of this address as the 1998 Chaim Weizmann Memorial Lecture in the Humanities, at the Weizmann Institute, Rehovot, Israel. This text was prepared in the last month or two of a year-long sabbatical leave as a Fellow of the Stanford Humanities Center. I thank the Director, Keith Baker, and his staff, for their many kindnesses.

1. Amos Elon, *A Blood-Dimmed Tide: Dispatches From the Middle East* (New York, 1997), p. 28.

2. Yaakov Shabtai, *Past Continuous,* trans. by Dalya Bilu (Philadelphia, 1983), pp. 38–39.

3. Derek Jonathan Penslar, "Innovation and Revisionism in Israeli Historiography," *History and Memory*, vol. 7, no. 1, Spring/Summer 1995, pp. 126–128.

4. Yaron Ezrahi, *Rubber Bullets: Power and Conscience in Modern Israel* (New York, 1996).

5. For an example of a recent, unremittingly bleak portrait of Ben Gurion, see Idith Zertal, *From Catastrophe to Power* (Berkeley, 1998). The standard biography is Shabtai Teveth, *Ben-Gurion* (Boston, 1987), highly detailed and alas, all too defensive.

6. Amos Oz, *Israel, Palestine and Peace: Essays* (San Diego, New York, 1994), pp. 50–51.

7. Gabriel Sheffer, *Moshe Sharett: Biography of a Political Moderate* (Oxford, 1996).

8. See the *Journal of Palestine Studies*, vol. 26, no. 4, Summer 1997.

9. Benny Morris, *The Birth of the Palestine Refugee Problem, 1947–1949* (Cambridge, 1987); Ilan Pappe, *The Making of the Arab-Israeli Conflict* (London, 1992). For an insightful review of the more standard works on Arabs and Zionism, see Joseph Heller, "Zionism and the Arab Question," *Studies in Contemporary Jewry*, vol. 4 (New York, 1988), pp. 295–304.

10. Uri Savir, *The Process* (New York, 1998), p. 15.

11. Penslar, "Innovation and Revisionism," p. 135.

12. Irving Howe, "The Age of Conformity," *Selected Essays, 1950–1990* (San Diego, New York, 1990), p. 36.

13. For an assessment of this body of literature from a rather different perspective, see Alvin H. Rosenfeld, "Promised Land(s): Zion, America, and American Jewish Writers," *Jewish Social Studies*, vol. 3, no. 3, new series, 1997, pp. 111–131.

14. Ruth R. Wisse, *If I Am Not for Myself?* (New York, 1992); Philip Roth, *The Counterlife* (New York, 1986); Philip Roth, *Operation Shylock* (New York, 1993).

15. Tova Reich, *The Jewish War* (New York, 1995).

16. Robert Stone, *Damascus Gate* (Boston, 1998).

17. Hugh Nissenson, *Notes From the Frontier* (New York, 1968), p. 70.

18. Tom Nairn, *Faces of Nationalism* (London, 1997), p. 121.

19. See the discussion of this point in Matthew D'Ancona's review of *Faces of Nationalism*, in *New Statesman*, vol. 127, no. 4376, March 12, 1998.

20. Tony Judt, *The Burden of Responsibility* (Chicago, 1998), p. 131.

21. Yael Tamir, *Liberal Nationalism* (Princeton, 1993), p. 6.

22. Meir Shalev, *The Blue Mountain*, trans. by Hillel Halkin (New York, 1991), p. 145.

INDIVIDUALISM AND COLLECTIVISM IN ZIONIST CULTURE AND THE STATE OF ISRAEL

Yaron Ezrahi

Bhikhu Parekh, in an essay titled "The Cultural Particularity of Liberal Democracy,"[1] argues that liberal democracy as a political system is a dialectical welding of two not fully compatible elements, of which liberalism is less universalistic, less well received, and less deployable than democracy. The claim that the individual is primary and the community is derivative is more controversial than the value or the application of democratic procedures such as free elections. In every society, there is a different balance between the liberal and democratic components, the rights and powers of citizens as individuals or members of minority groups, and the rights and powers of the state and the majority that controls the instruments of government.

During the last two and a half centuries, the encounter between liberalism and nationalism or clericalism has found the Jews mostly on the liberal side, as articulate protagonists of individual freedoms and minority rights. The affinities of Jewish intellectuals to cosmopolitan enlightenment ideas has come to be regarded as a special characteristic of Jewish secular culture and the Jewish intelligentsia.[2]

This tendency has raised expectations that a Jewish polity will rest on liberal principles and uphold the fundamental commitments to a bill of rights and principles of equality. In light of this tendency and such expectations, how can we account for the fact that Israel, the "Jewish state," has no constitution, no bill of rights, a dismal record of discrimination against non-Jewish minorities (particularly Arabs and Druzes), and a hegemonic religion—an established church with the political power to divert massive public resources to support religious education and limit civic education in the Israeli school system? How can we account for the weakness of the liberal component in the Israeli democracy, the death of the Israeli liberal party, the loneliness of the Israeli supreme court as the custodian of individual rights, and the feeble checks on arbitrary uses of state powers vis-à-vis Jews and non-Jews alike?

This state of affairs is not only at odds with Jewish liberalism in the Diaspora but also with powerful liberal ideas which can be found in classical Hebrew texts. The present alliance of both the orthodox and ultra-orthodox Jewish establishments with the nationalist block obscures other currently neglected strains of Jewish religious culture. Several scholars, including most recently Aviezer Ravitzky and Menahem Loberbaum, have shown the depth and the richness of the rabbinical traditions generally espousing secularized conceptions of politics. Maimonides, Adret and Gerondi—for instance—stressed the limits of the Torah in guiding the handling of ordinary affairs, allowing considerable freedom for pragmatic flexibility.[3] Moshe Idel insists that the rabbinical, rationalist, individualist strain in Judaism is marginal in relation to the mythological, mystical, and irrational components of the Jewish religious worldview and practice. This in itself, however, need not rule out circumstances or historical forces that can select and elevate the marginal over the mainstream. Therefore, those who seek support for liberal individualism in Jewish classical texts and Jewish general culture need not despair. Some sources even seem to anticipate specific liberal ideas such as the primacy of the individual. Shalom Albeck argues, for instance, that according to Alfasi (1013–1103), his student Ibn Migas (1077–1141), and later, Meir Abulafia (1170–1244), "the community is not a legal persona distinct from its members but rather a partnership of individuals."[4]

Despite the persistent power of the idea of the "people," the Jewish collective, in Judaism tensions between individual and community are present in various spheres of Jewish culture. The absence of a powerful liberal/individualistic component in what emerged as the modern Jewish state cannot be accounted for by the absence of religious, cultural, or historical resources that could be relied on and developed to support it. While I do not wish to belittle the power of collectivism in Judaism both as religion and as culture, the explanation for the weakness of the liberal element in the modern Jewish state seems to lie elsewhere.

In some of the great liberal traditions of western Europe, such as the English or the French, the liberal impulse to protect individual citizens against arbitrary use of coercive state power grew largely from a history of domestic conflicts and civil wars between governors and their own subjects, citizens, and their own states. Jews were vulnerable, of course, to such abusive state powers but not from their own state. Their enemies were not their own governors. The history of Jewish statelessness and powerlessness has, therefore, encouraged romantic and even mystical notions of Jewish military force, notions blind to the dangers inherent in such force in a Jewish polity. Instead, Israelis and many Diaspora Jews have come to view the power of the state as the actual or symbolic embodiment of their freedom, not as a potential threat to their liberties. For decades, Israeli secret services have kindled the enthusiasm and fantasies of millions of Jews in Israel and around the world. This was only one symptom of a more general celebratory, romantic orientation towards Jewish power and its agents. In this climate, Israelis were unable to develop the vital liberal culture of ambivalence and guardedness towards the power of their own state, the ambivalence and suspicion that in other societies have encouraged the internal evolution of constitutional constraints on the uses of state powers.

Until very recently, the editors of Israeli daily newspapers collaborated with the state in imposing on their newspapers voluntary self-censorship. For years, the focus on the use of force vis-à-vis non-Jews outside and inside Israel retarded the development of liberal sensibilities and internal legal, institutional, and ethical limits on the uses of state powers. In the absence of a sociopolitical support system, Israel developed as a lean procedural/institutional democracy. The fragility of the Israeli liberal/constitutional structure was revealed even before the assassination of Prime Minister Rabin in November 1995, and the events that led to it, by the frivolous tinkering with the electoral law introducing a clause for the direct elections of the prime minister, which put Israel—in comparative classifications—in the family of Latin-American regimes. In May 1996, with the first direct election of its prime minister, Israel stopped being a parliamentary democracy. I would like to suggest that in this context, without constitutional checks and balances, the introduction of a majority rule or a mass vote, which limits the scope and authority of proportional representation, was a dangerous victory of anti-parliamentary, populistic politics over the liberal element in Israeli politics. In a country where the organic notion of peoplehood is so deeply rooted, majoritarianism combined with ethnic, religious com-munitarianism could pose a direct threat to such vital institu-tions as the Supreme Court.[5]

Another contributing factor to the weakness of the liberal element in the Israeli polity is the obvious fact that the Zionist enterprise was developed historically as a national liberation project, in the context of which the emancipation of the Jew as an individual was a derivative idea and for a long time a practical impossibility. The stress on the return and liberation of the Jewish people to their homeland actually turned the individual into a missionary of the group. Settlement, con-quest, war, the development of a military ethos, nation-build-ing, and the like are not typical liberal objectives, nor are they the kinds of projects that reinforce a commitment to liberal values or the cultivation of liberal sensibilities. Communitari-anism was much more effective and functional than liberalism in supporting the extractive policies of the state in the decades of nation-building. Liberalism has been more relevant as an ideological and political resource in the more limited context of evolving a modern legal framework for the new state, which claimed a place in the family of enlightened modern democra-cies. The primary preoccupations of the new immigrant soci-ety of Israel before the establishment of the state in May 1948 (and even more so since) were with how to develop physical force that would be sufficiently effective to uphold the found-ing and survival of the new state and with how to legitimate its uses. Here socialism and nationalism were, of course, much more relevant frames.

Inspired by the Russian Revolution, Socialist Zionists from Eastern Europe were the carriers of a tradition that rested on ethical justifications for the use of force in the pursuit of an ideal society. In the context of Zionism, socialism had a special appeal in providing, among other things, a universalist/ethical rationale for the uses of force in the service of pragmatic nationalism. On the other side of the political spectrum, Nationalist Zionists evolved a Jewish version of the particularistic rationale of violence as a means of group survival. Drawing on Darwin, Spencer, and "real politique" doctrines, Nationalist Jewish intellectuals like Jabotinsky laid the foundations for the idealization of the Jewish army as a means of survival and liberation. By dramatically internationalizing the tragedy of Jewish victimhood, the Holocaust in fact expanded if not fully universalized the justification of Jewish national aspirations and the nationalist rationale for the use of violence. With its establishment, the state of Israel was presented and perceived as a state of former victims with a mandate to redress a historical injustice to the Jewish people. Since 1948, the Israeli Leviathan has turned out to be one of the most demanding and extractive states in modern times, relying on the radical sacrifices of blood, sweat, and money from its tiny population. Liberal ideas and practices that were imported to Israel by Jewish immigrants from Germany, Western Europe, and other countries did not survive for long, although some did find enduring expression in the tradition of the Israeli Supreme Court and in the development of financial and commercial institutions.

In the atmosphere of nation-building, the absorption of mass immigration (mostly from poor countries), and the state of almost permanent war with the Arabs, liberal individualism could not be attractive or a feasible practice. It was identified with the negative values that appeared opposed to Israeli communal idealism. As compared to Israeli patriotism, asceticism, self-sacrifice, military prowess, group solidarity, Aliya, and the like, individualism came to represent self-indulgent hedonism, egoistic materialism, legal formalism, and migration to affluent societies like America and Canada. Perhaps more important was the fact that in the context of a Jewish state directed by a Jewish majority, Jews lost the political motive to seek emancipation as individuals that had nourished their liberalism in societies hostile to the development of their collective ethnic, religious, and cultural identities. In the Israeli context, classical liberal ideas of individual and minority rights appeared to serve the claims of non-Jewish minorities and therefore provide rationales for limiting the powers of the Jewish majority. In the context of Israeli politics, liberalism came to rival Jewish nationalism.

In retrospect, it is clear now that Israeli/Zionist collectivism rested on very fragile foundations. Zionism was essentially a syncretic movement based on a temporary truce between socialist, nationalist, liberal, religious, and secular Zionists, and between Western and Eastern cultural outlooks. During the first decades of statehood, this pluralism was restrained by the enormity of the tasks of survival and nation-building. But with the consolidation of Israeli security and economy, the stabilization of Israel's place among nations, and the necessity of facing hard choices with respect to the Palestinians, the surface consensus started to erode rapidly. Israel's public life has come to center on a series of controversies about wars that appeared unnecessary; an occupation that appeared to an increasing number of Israelis as corruptive and untenable; failed leaders who encouraged the spread of distrust in the government; the assassination of a prime minister; the issue of the peace with the Palestinians; the place of religion and religious authority in the state of Israel; and the widening gap between the rich and poor. These developments, and particularly the breakdown of the thin consensus between the secular Left and the secular Right on issues of war, territories, and peace, opened the political system for the ascent of the religious parties and their ability to translate their political power into an effective assault on civic education and secular culture as well as on the bastion of Israeli liberal values, the Supreme Court. During years of right-wing governments culminating in the government headed by Benjamin Netanyahu (1996-1999), the great-grandchildren of the early secular Zionists who rebelled against traditional religious culture were waging a defensive cultural and institutional battle against a powerful front of the descendants of the Jewish fundamentalist reaction against Zionism and their right-wing Zionist allies.

In this context, Israel has evolved a brand of secular individualism, or rather secular singlehood, which unlike the richer and deeper forms of liberal selfhood that evolve slowly from an internal culture of spiritual, ethical, and intellectual individualism, results from the collapse and fragmentation of collective frames of meaning. In this Israeli universe, the individual is more a survivor of a collective that lost its force, a fragment of a former whole, than a rich albeit small whole unto itself. This is not yet the kind of liberal individualism that can uphold a liberal society and liberal democratic institutions or generate the sensibilities and cultural forms of a universe nourished by forces unleashed by newly acquired freedoms. This is not yet the kind of pluralistic, internally open, mobile, and tolerant individualism that is upheld in a liberal/democratic state by a culture of inherently unsettled meaning, a culture that rests on a dynamic core of what William E. Connolly has aptly called "productive ambiguity." This is a condition that literally disempowers the state in its attempts to ground power and authority in a hegemonic, institutionalized, cultural, and normative frame.[6] Despite these limitations, however, along with the consolidation of a new Israeli fundamentalist identity, the most significant force working within and reshaping Israeli culture today amid the ruins of broken collectivist utopias is the increasingly articulate expression of individualism.

In the early decades of statehood, sporadic expressions of individuality were bound to emerge through friction with collective expectations and trigger pressures for group conformity. But with the relaxation of such external communal sanctions in recent years, the focus seems to have been gradually shifting to more internal domains expressing the urge to escape the oppressive gaze of the collective. At present, the new Israeli self seems at a loss to marshal the strength and the skills to transcend one-dimensional singlehood of the kind produced by fragmentation of collectives and to evolve an internally cultivated and therefore more attractive normative individualism.

Decades of redemptive epic politics of sacrifice and normative Zionist collectivism have created in Israel generations of Jews cut off from what Michel Foucault aptly called "technologies of the self." These are the tools and strategies that have been developing for centuries, especially in Western societies, to form selves differentiated from collective, often hidden, clusters of communal consciousness and power, individuals free from fantasies of spontaneous, holistic social harmonies.

Without such techniques and without visions of selfhood as a positive program (not just the relic of a ruined community), Israeli or for that matter any democracy cannot flourish. Even if we acknowledge with Emil Durkheim that individualism depends on socially generated structures of significance that repudiate the idea of essentialist liberal individualism, liberal individualism remains a potent political strategy of democratization. The question remains, however: From where could Israeli individuals draw the models, the motives, and the strength to assume responsibility for fixing the meaning of individual life, the courage to engage in self-narration rather than to be attached to precast frames of life? A viable Israeli individualism that can generate or uphold commitments to democratic civil society and can hold its own in the face of the pressures of coercive communitarian norms cannot be imported, nor can it be sustained on the basis of a culturally impoverished economic egoism. Like English, French, and American individualism, Israeli individualism must be forged from local materials within its own particular society.

The Israeli individual cannot escape the arduous task of negotiating the cultural, psychological, political, legal, and spiritual spaces within which it can define itself and develop. Israeli individualism cannot evolve without reckoning with constraints such as Israeli/Jewish essentialist or organic conceptions of peoplehood, the rejection of the liberal democratic notion of *majority* as an aggregate of all individual citizens and therefore inclusive of non-Jews, the influence of the Israeli military ethos, or the political chains that arrest changes in Israeli education. Its future will depend largely on its capacity to draw upon indigenous Israeli cultural materials such as Hebrew poetry, art, progressive religious thinkers, etc.

Such Israeli individualism may first have to go through a phase of flat individualism—what I called *singlehood*—before it could go on to the richer phase based on the democratization of uniqueness and pluralistic selfhood. The earlier expectations that liberal individualism will evolve and spread as a universal phenomenon, a logically necessary phase in the process of modernization, was based on false enlightenment conceptions of politics and history. Many intellectual historians and political theorists have regarded individualism as a necessary or at least probable development concomitant with the transition of *gemeinschaft* to *gesellschaft*, traditional community to society, and as an aspect of modernization as a universal process of rationalization of culture, society, and politics.

We understand better today that the intellectual history of complex processes such as the genealogy of individualism is too narrow and incomplete without, say, the history of group emotions and their social expressions. Israel may be a case in point. When the history of Israeli individualism is written at some future date, I trust that the development as well as the changing expressions of pain and emotional ambivalence in relation to the price of the Zionist project and the split among Israelis who could entertain the dual narratives of liberation and conquest as against those who could see only liberation or only conquest will be a very central chapter.

In the epic universe of monumental history, ambivalence is either absent or rare, and pain, if it is articulated at all, tends to be an abstract category. Pain denotes a different experience when it develops in conjunction with the emergence of individualism that redefines the loss of each individual life as irremediable.

A community conceived as the voluntary creation of discrete individuals develops a different notion of death and mourning than a community conceived as an organic whole in which individuals can be regarded as interchangeable extensions of the collective. The multiplicity of heterogeneous individual perspectives and the erosion of shared understandings of death in action raise the frightening possibility of meaningless death, meaningless pain. Nothing seems to limit the capacity of the state to mobilize its citizens and convince them to risk their lives for the collective more than the fear that the meaning of sacrifice, which appears glorious today, will be debased tomorrow, that those who died yesterday in a war of liberation will be remembered in the future as soldiers who died in a colonial war, or that the heroes who died in the last war will be remembered as victims or victimizers. When the structures of communal meaning attached to the goals of power and the sacrifices of the citizens are unstable, a war can be defended only on the much less culturally or religiously rich grounds of minimal security requirements.

Such a condition increases the burden of the state to provide acceptable justifications for risking the lives of its citizens in the battlefield. It is instructive to examine the shift marked, for instance, in the letters sent to bereaved families on Memorial Day by Begin, 1981 and Rabin, 1987.[7] Begin wrote: "On this Memorial Day all of us invoke the eternal memory of our heroes, those who redeemed Jerusalem." Rabin's language is very different. In 1987 he wrote: "I have no words to console you, to remedy your pain. I know that there are no words that can fill the emptiness created at your home...." Rabin's letter is responsive to a deep process of the individualization of pain in the course of the 1980s.

In the late 1990s, there is a widening rupture between the two outlooks on community pain and death, between mostly (but not only) religious Israeli youth who are highly motivated to fight and risk their lives for a communal notion of the land of Israel and a restored Jewish sovereignty, and Israeli youth who are much more skeptical and ambivalent with respect to this project and the anticipated costs in lives and suffering. The former seem to ally collectivism, patriotism, high fighting spirit, nationalism, religious outlook, and the willingness to overcome individual losses and pain. The latter seem to link individualism, a commitment to a peace settlement based on territorial compromises, liberal values, a secular outlook, and an unwillingness to suffer or inflict the losses and the pain involved. In a sense, then, one sign of the times has been the politicization of pain. While for one group the pain and suffering in the conflict has been enlisted to a defense of a more vigorous use of force, for the other individualization of pain and bereavement evolved as part of a process of distancing the individual from the community and questioning the costly missions of the state. While such differences in outlooks and orientations do not warrant simple dichotomies and the spectrum of attitudes is certainly much more complex than we can describe here, these distinctions are sufficiently significant to warrant close examination.

Among many types of illustrations and evidence, one can find these two outlooks compellingly articulated and juxtaposed in two photographs by Adi Nes showing in exhibitions of contemporary Israeli art at the Israel Museum in Jerusalem and the Jewish Museum in New York (1998–99). One photograph depicts a yarmulke-wearing Israeli soldier, apparently of Oriental background, flexing his muscles. The exposed part of his body seems to fully identify with the uniform. The other photograph shows a group of Ashkenzai-looking soldiers who appear somewhat hesitantly to be clapping for an unseen subject. They wear their uniforms loosely, and one of them allows his white T-shirt to show beneath his unbuttoned army shirt. A one-armed soldier who cannot clap his hands is sitting like a living statue in their midst, wearing his army trousers with only an undershirt on top. The undershirts seem to challenge the uniform just as the private person within resists the soldier without. Together, the two photographs convey the widening gulf between ambivalent and unambivalent attitudes towards the use of military force in contemporary Israel.

Jonathan Mandell, who reviewed the exhibition (significantly entitled "After Rabin") for *Newsday*,[8] reports that when Avi Nes's religious soldier was shown at the Israel museum in Jerusalem, several American tourists asked whether they could get a postcard of it, "mistaking it for an unironic symbol of a New Israel." The power of irony and ambivalence to expose the uncertain relations between death and meaning is, of course, one of the most subversive strategies of art as political criticism. It reveals the very gaps that undermine the power of the state to mobilize the sacrifices of its citizens. In Israel, where religion and ideology have long competed regarding the sacralization of all aspects of society, Israeli artists have been evolving a profane, emotional, aesthetic culture of irony and ambivalence in which the Israeli self can increasingly discover the rich options that lie between messianic enthusiasm and melancholy. Such ambiguities, the underdeterminism of meaning inseparable from the rise of modern and, even more, post-modern individualism, often appear threatening to conservatives like Michel Sandel. They worry about "the drift to formless Protean storyless selves, unable to weave the various strands of their identity into a coherent whole."[9] But at this time, Israeli artists see the breakdown of such a coherent whole as opening the way for emancipation into a new kind of freedom.

Larry Abramson, an Israeli painter, has perhaps captured the particular mood of contemporary Israelis who try to write poetry, paint, or compose, standing in what looks like a junkyard of broken utopias. "The family cell of Israeli art," he observed, "the family parented by both Zionism and modernism has long disintegrated. We Israeli artists are orphans, we have no family, no name, no home, no purpose…[we] learn to grow up alone and take full responsibility for our lives. The abandoned children are condemned to make meaning from scratch from nothing and form a critical voluntary community out of a haphazard assortment of homeless. Eventually, everyone will discover that he or she are orphans…The citizens will lift off the burdens of pre-cast truths and will turn to the artist-orphans for guidance. The future belongs to the orphans."[10] Abramson's imprinting of oil paintings on newspaper is suggestive of the dialectics of effacement and creation, concealment and expression of the Israeli experience.

If Abramson dwells upon the ironies of the dualism between seeing and not seeing, painting and effacing, another leading Israeli artist, Nurit David, explores the deepest personal sources of subjectivity by focusing on being and disappearing. In her paintings, almost everything occurs in the stairroom in what she says is "not a real place but a surfing site, an experience of constant fluctuations between appearance and disappearance."[11]

At the moment, to be an Israeli Jew has become very much like moving up and down the stairs in this mediating space in which nothing is settled or predictable. To be an Israeli is, at least for secular Israelis, increasingly an act of improvisation, of trying, exploring, experimenting, and moving between several possible spaces and identities. It is hardly conceivable, not even desirable of course, that liberal individualism or its post-modern mutations could ever become a total alternative to Israeli collectivisms. The question is more whether Israel can grow to accommodate individualism grounded in a rich culture of the self, a universe of diverse and assertive subjectivities that can provide a normative base for individualism as a check on coercive statist and communitarian powers and authority.

Presently, the incipient Israeli individualism co-exists tensely with fundamentalist Jewish identities for whom Israel as a place is a primordial given and Jewish fate is inescapable. But the future will belong neither to the orphans nor to the children of Israel. It will largely consist of what the children of Israel who declare themselves orphans and those who worship their fathers will do or not do to negotiate the terms of their coexistence. At the moment, however, the stair-room does not connect to the apartments, and those locked up safely in their apartments do not open their doors to the stair-room.

Theoretically, one of the most potent liberal critiques of nationalism is that the very act of creating state power precedes the expression of the very will that can legitimate it. It is therefore a case of power that fixes and protects the very system of meaning that in turn legitimates it. The only defense against arbitrary power is therefore in the liberal view, to dismantle the encompassing social structure of significance that legitimates power, to disrupt the tyranny of supposedly shared meaning, and to divide and subdivide power. David Quint, in his brilliant *Epic and Empire*,[12] refers to the role of power in the selection and shaping of the narratives of communal lives in his discussion of Virgil's Aeneid. While empires have, according to Quint, the power to narrate history as an epic, minor powers and losers must accommodate contingencies. Unlike the defeated, victors experience history as a coherent story directed by collective will. Liberals might reverse this order, making the real winners all the citizens who are freed from experiencing history as a coherent, single, celebratory, master narrative.

Notes

1. Bhikhu Parekh, "The Cultural Particularity of Liberal Democracy," in *Prospects For Democracy*, David Held (ed.) (Cambridge, Polity Press, 1993), pp. 156–175.

2. Yaron Ezrahi, *Rubber Bullets: Power and Conscience in Modern Israel* (New York, Farrar Straus and Giraux, 1997).

3. Menachem Lorberbaum, *Secularizing Politics in Medieval Jewish Thought* (forthcoming).

4. Ibid.

5. Attempts to repeal or modify the law that introduced the direct election of the Prime Minister in Israel are continuing all the time.

6. William E. Connolly, *Identity\Difference Democratic Negotiations of Political Paradox* (Ithaca and London, Cornell Univ. Press, 1991), chapter 7.

7. I draw here on an unpublished study by Shaul Shenhav.

8. *Newsday* (September 11, 1998).

9. Michael J. Sandel, *Democracy's Discontent* (Cambridge Mass, Harvard University Press, 1996), pp. 350–351.

10. *StudioArt Magazine* (In Hebrew), vol. 94, June-July 1998, pp. 16–19.

11. Ibid., pp. 21–30.

12. David Quint, *Epic and Empire* (Princeton, Princeton University Press, 1993).

ZIONISM AND
THE ARAB WORLD

Itamar Rabinovich

In 1905, Najib Azoury, a Lebanese Christian political activist exiled in Paris, published a book-cum-political manifesto titled *Le Reveil de la nation arabe dans l'Asie turque.* In it Azoury wrote the following paragraph:

> Two important phenomena, of the same nature and yet opposed to one another, which have not yet attracted the attention of anyone, are manifesting themselves at this moment in Asiatic Turkey: they are the awakening of the Arab nation and the hidden effort of the Jews to establish on a very grand scale the ancient monarchy of Israel. These two movements are destined to fight each other continually, until one of the two prevails. On the final result of this struggle between the two peoples, representing two opposing principles, hinges the destiny of the entire world.[1]

Azoury was a minor adventurer, operating at the margins of French politics and policy-making. He made this observation when Arab nationalism, Zionism, the modern Jewish community in Palestine, and the antagonism between Jews and Arabs on its soil were in their infancy. Under these circumstances, Azoury's ability to identify the potential inherent in both movements and in the conflict between them, his hyperbolic final sentence notwithstanding, is striking.[2]

Azoury realized that at issue was a clash of two nationalisms. He was right to conclude that given the pan-Arab and Islamic dimensions of Arab nationalism, the Jewish people's

47

dispersion around the world, and Palestine's geopolitical and religious significance, the Arab-Jewish dispute in Palestine could not remain a local issue. During much of the preceding century it seemed that he was also right in depicting the conflict as insoluble, a collision between two irreconcilable protagonists. But this paper will argue that what had been true for so many decades is no longer valid, that the Oslo Accords laid the ground for a historic compromise between the two national movements. It will argue further that it is precisely this prospect and the concomitant need on both sides to make painful choices and to face internal dissension that make the present phase more difficult than earlier phases when the lines were drawn clearly and objectives rested on a broad consensus.

The term *Zionism,* as used here, refers to the ideology of Jewish nationalism and Jewish statehood in Palestine as the ancestral home of the Jewish people, to the movement that carried it, and to the Jewish community in prestate Israel. A Zionist movement has continued to exist after the formation of the Jewish state but it was replaced in May 1948 by the State of Israel as a protagonist in the conflict. The Arab World can be an amorphous term; Zionism's equivalent on the other side of the conflict have been the ideas of Arab, pan-Arab, and Palestinian Arab nationalism and the regimes, movements, and institutions through which they have been expressed.

Before dealing with the prospects of compromise and accommodation between Zionism and the Arab world, it is important to review the evolution of their conflict as it proceeded through five principal phases.

The Early Years, 1882 to 1917

Much happened during these three and a half decades. Modern Jewish settlements were established in Palestine, and two waves of immigration infused new blood into the "old Yishuv," as the Jewish community in Ottoman Palestine was called. The Zionist movement was formed, and several key decisions regarding its program, orientation, and actual conduct were taken. Most of the Arab world as we know it now was still part of the Ottoman Empire. Most Arabs still thought of identity and politics in traditional terms—religious, dynastic and local. But modern ideas of nationalism arrived on the scene, prominently among them the idea of Arab nationalism. The scholarship of the last three decades dispelled two widely held assumptions about this period. One held that early Zionism had ignored or disregarded "the Arab question," that it acted under the slogan "a land without people to a people without a land." According to this view, Yitzhak Epshtein, an intellectual who had arrived in Palestine as part of the "First Aliyya," published his essay "A Hidden Question" in 1907 in order to alert his fellow Zionists to the existence of "an Arab problem" they would rather ignore.

But this is a misrepresentation of Epshtein's essay. Epshtein did not start a discussion of a hitherto latent issue but joined a debate on this very issue that had begun earlier and was intensified on the eve of World War I. The Zionist leadership in Europe and the members of the small Jewish community in Palestine were fully aware of the demographic realities on the ground and of the actual and potential Arab opposition to large-scale Jewish immigration and settlement, let alone statehood.[3]

Another related assumption held sway for many years—
that there was no initial Arab opposition to the fresh waves of
Jewish immigration and to the establishment of new Jewish
settlements and that opposition erupted only after the publication of the Balfour Declaration in November, 1917. A
review of archives, the contemporary press, and several memoirs readily showed that various elements in Arab society—
agricultural workers worried about competition, politically
conscious urban populations worried by the far-reaching ramifications of the Jewish return to Zion—manifested their hostility to Jewish immigrants and settlers and to the Zionist
idea.[4]

Yet, both phenomena—Zionist awareness of Arab presence and antagonism in Palestine and the extent and level of
that antagonism—must not be overstated. Arab nationalism
prior to World War I, certainly prior to 1908, was an incipient
force, and the notion of an Arab Palestine as a distinct political
entity had yet to emerge (ironically, its subsequent emergence
was to some extent a by-product of the conflict with Zionism).[5] Opposition to Zionist ideas and activities was sporadic,
localized, and unfocused, and the Zionist movement, as a con-
sequence, was not forced to come to grips with it. A full-
fledged Arab-Zionist conflict developed only in the aftermath
of World War I, and it was the destruction of the Ottoman
Empire and the post-war peace settlement in the Middle East
that set the stage for it.

The Arab-Jewish Conflict in and over Palestine, 1918 to 1948

The course of World War I, the wartime diplomacy, and the
postwar settlement fashioned Palestine west of the Jordan as a

British Mandate dedicated both to the establishment of a Jewish national home in Palestine and to the protection of the Arab population's rights. The arena was thus defined for a struggle between the Jewish community, supported by the Zionist movement and the bulk of the Jewish people, and the Arab community, supported by the larger Arab world and part of the Muslim world, over the right to and control of Palestine.[6] After nearly thirty years of conflict, the international community, through a UN vote, tried to resolve the issue through partition but failed. The Jewish side accepted the resolution; the Arab side refused. A civil war in Palestine ensued, followed by an Arab-Israeli war that ended in Israeli victory, the consolidation of Jewish statehood over a larger territory, and the fragmentation and dispersion of the Palestinian community.

During this period, there was no single Zionist view of the conflict with the Palestinian Arabs and the larger Arab world, but a whole gamut of opinion stretching from liberal belief in the idea of a binational state through several varieties of socialist and religious Zionism to bourgeois and nationalist maximalist Zionism.[7] By the mid-1930s, the centrist wing of Labor Zionism headed by David Ben-Gurion established the hegemony it enjoyed for the next forty years. For practical purposes our attention should focus on this dominant school and on the dichotomy between it and the Revisionist right wing.

The mainstream Zionist leadership sought Jewish statehood; it also sought agreement with Palestinian Arab nationalism and accepted the principle of partition in 1937. Ben Gurion authorized further contacts and negotiations even though he had reached the conclusion that the Arab world would not agree to partition and that war with the Palestinian Arabs and the Arab states was inevitable.[8]

The Zionist leadership had an ambivalent view of pan-Arab nationalism. If Jewish statehood was unacceptable to the Arab world and a collision was inevitable, the formation of a large, powerful Arab entity was a threatening prospect. But there was also a different current in Zionist thinking, which argued that it would be impossible to reach a compromise with Palestinian Arab nationalism in a dispute over Palestine's small territory; but if a large Arab entity—a union or a federation—were to be formed, its leaders would conceivably be more likely to come to a compromise with the Zionist leadership. This stance was evident in Chaim Weizmann's meeting with Amir Faysal in 1919 and in the Zionist attitude toward the various Arab unity schemes in the 1940s.[9]

On a different level, Zionist diplomacy dealt with the neighboring Arab states—Egypt, Transjordan, Syria, and Lebanon—seeking to form partnerships and alliances or, at least, to prevent them from joining the looming war.

Zionism's Revisionist wing (and for that matter, though for different reasons, other Zionist groups) was opposed to any territorial concessions. Palestine, the Land of Israel, on both sides of the Jordan was the Jewish people's homeland and the Jewish State must encompass all of it. The Palestinian Arabs who resided in it would enjoy full civic rights but no national rights. Arab nationalism was not a force that had to be reckoned with.

The Arab view of Zionism was dark and stark. In the 1920s, a Palestinian Arab nationalist movement emerged that viewed Zionism as its nemesis. The movement was dominated by its radical wing, which saw any concession and compromise as heresy and treason. This trend was reinforced by the victory of a radical version of pan-Arab nationalism over the territorial nationalist ideas in Egypt and Lebanon and over the pragmatic Hashemite version of Arab nationalism.

For the triumphant brand of Arab nationalism, Zionism was an alien invader—part of the colonial European invasion that subjugated much of the Arab world in the aftermath of World War I. Radical Arab nationalists in Syria and Iraq may have lacked the direct contact with the Jewish community that the Palestinians had, but for them, the Zionist challenge to Arab Palestine became one of Arabism's most important defining issues.[10]

In 1936 the British government invited the Arab states to exercise restraining influence over the rebellious Palestinian Arabs. In 1939 it invited them to participate together with the Palestinian Arab and Jewish delegations at the St. James Conference in London to seek a political settlement to the Palestine conflict. On the eve of World War II, Britain published a White Paper that tilted toward the Arab side in the conflict in order to attract the Arab world's support in the impending war. These were all milestones on the path that led the Arab states to a full involvement in the conflict. As a by-product of this development, the Palestinians lost control over the course of events; the decisions affecting their future were now made by the more powerful Arab states. The latter were in turn drawn to a war that some of them did not want. But the interplay of state interests, inter-Arab rivalries, and ideological commitment led them to stage the invasion of Israel in May 15, 1948.

Elusive Peace: 1948 to 1967

The establishment of the State of Israel and its victory in the 1948 war marked the implementation of Zionism's principal goal but presented the leadership of the new state with a whole host of fresh problems. The character of the new state had to be defined, as well as its relationship with the majority of the Jewish people that continued to live in the Diaspora. Relations with the Arab world were one of the young state's most cardinal problems. That relationship had three principal dimensions: relations with an Arab (Palestinian) minority of 11 percent, relations with the other components of the fragmented and dispersed Palestinian people, and relations with the defeated Arab states.

All efforts to end the 1948 war with a peace settlement failed. To the Israelis, the Arabs were a defeated aggressor. Israel had accepted the United Nations' partition resolution, but the Arabs had refused to accept it, launched war, and lost; why should Israel reward aggression? Furthermore, even in the larger territory it controlled at the war's end, Israel faced an impossible challenge. The Arabs insisted on territorial concessions and on the return of the Palestinian refugees. But their attack in 1948 had demonstrated that Israel faced a very real existential challenge; it simply could not afford such concessions. Peace was a high Israeli priority, but not at any price. The status quo could be consolidated through armistice agreement, and formal peace should be available to Israel on better terms a few years later.

From the Arab perspective, Israel was an illegitimate entity, forced on the Arabs and planted in their midst by Western colonialism and by force. A terrible injustice may have been caused to the Jews in Europe, but why should the Arabs be made to pay for it? The original sin of Israel's very creation was compounded by the injustice and suffering that had been inflicted on the Palestinians. They ended up stateless, fragmented, and dispersed. Nothing could make up for this injustice but if an Arab state or the Arab states were to come to Israel, let Israel pay a visibly painful price—take back the Palestinian refugees, give up the Southern Negev or half of Lake Tiberias, or offer a corridor linking Gaza to the West Bank. Since Israel won the war and was militarily superior, there was no choice for the Arabs but to sign armistice agreements with the Jewish state. But formal peace treaties legitimizing the illegitimate state were a different issue.[11]

The gap that separated these outlooks was at the core of the stalemate, which lasted from 1949 to 1967. Stalemate led to festering,[12] and by the mid-1950s the full-fledged Arab-Israeli conflict was in place. The total Arab boycott, the political and diplomatic campaign, and the ever-present danger of another war became governing factors of Israeli life.

This was matched by the centrality of the conflict with Israel to the Arab world. The Palestinians were a secondary actor during most of this period: They were traumatized and dispersed, and their leadership was discredited by failure. Until the emergence of new Palestinian leadership and activism in the mid-1960s, most Palestinians tended to identify with pan-Arab nationalism and to expect their own redemption as part of the Arab nation's unity and renaissance.

Indeed, on the Arab side, the period's most important development was the rise of Nasserism—a messianic, pan-Arab nationalist movement predicated on the power of the Egyptian state and the charismatic personality of Gamal Abdul Nasser. Nasserism galvanized the familiar elements of the Arab position toward Israel and supplemented them with new ones. Israel was a geopolitical obstacle separating Egypt from the eastern part of the Arab world. It was a western implant in the

Arab world, an ally of the West and the conservative Arabs. As Nasser's regime drifted to the left and close to the Soviet Union, his hostility to Israel was couched in stronger ideological terms. When Nasserism reached its zenith (1958 to 1961), Arab expectations of defeating Israel through unified Arab action soured. Its decline and the exacerbation of "the Arab cold war" in the mid-1960s contributed to the outbreak of the Six Day War in June 1967.[13]

1967 to 1993

The Six Day War was a watershed in the evolution of Israel's relationship with the Arab world. Its impact has been mixed. By providing Israel with territorial assets that could be used in "land for peace" agreements and by demonstrating Israel's clear military superiority, it laid the foundations for the peace process that began six years later. But it also released in Israel a wave of messianic nationalism that turned the West Bank into a new arena of Israeli-Palestinian and therefore Israeli-Arab confrontation.

Three Arab states—Egypt, Syria and Jordan—lost territory to Israel in the June 1967 war. Jordan stood in a category by itself; its annexation of the West Bank had been controversial. Israel, while acknowledging Egyptian and Syrian sovereignty over the Sinai and the Golan, maintained that sovereignty over the West Bank was an open issue, and the Palestinian nationalists, now assembled under the Palestine Liberation Organization's umbrella, argued that Palestine was the legitimate Arab contender for the West Bank.

The war's impact on Egypt and Syria unfolded in two phases. The loss of national territory created a new level of involvement in the conflict for both countries. Solidarity with the Palestinian cause and commitment to Arab nationalism's view of Israel were one thing, but the loss of national territory was another. Egypt's six-year effort through the war of attrition and the October War and Syria's ongoing effort have reflected this new level of commitment. But Egypt in 1977 and Syria in 1993 expressed their willingness to offer Israel full contractual peace in exchange for a full withdrawal from the Sinai and the Golan. These two paragons of Arab nationalism thus separated themselves, albeit temporarily, from the Palestinian cause. But as will be seen later, a new linkage was established, at least in Egypt's case, between the Palestinian issue and the level of peace with Israel. Jordan announced its disengagement from the West Bank and endorsed Israel's agreement with the PLO, but with a Palestinian majority on its soil, it remains intimately linked to the Palestinian issue.

In the evolution of the Palestinian issue, 1967 marked a crucial turning point. Israel's victory brought the whole of Palestine west of the Jordan under a single authority for the first time since 1948. Conceivably, the partition that had not been implemented in 1947 could be effected now by a victorious and powerful Israel, but conditions were not ripe for such a compromise. Instead, another phase of the Israeli-Palestinian dispute was launched.

The Palestinian side in this conflict was led by the PLO. The organization had been formed by the Arab states in 1964 but was taken over in 1968 by the authentic Palestinian organizations that had surfaced in the mid-1960s. Against the background of the Arab regimes' and Arab regular armies' failure in 1967, the PLO as a nationalist movement advocating guerrilla warfare acquired the prestige and influence in the Arab world that the Palestinians had lacked so glaringly in earlier decades. The PLO and its constituent organizations fought against Israel on many fronts—from Lebanon and Jordan, on the West Bank and the Gaza Strip, and through terrorist acts in Israel itself and around the globe.

When the Arab-Israeli peace process began at the end of 1973, the PLO had to formulate its own position regarding the prospect of accommodation with Israel. It began to grapple with the issue in 1974, but it was only in 1988 that the PLO explicitly and fully accepted the notion of a two-state solution to the Palestinian-Israeli conflict.

During the previous twenty-two years Israeli politics, though, the concept of Zionism and Israel's view of the Palestinian issue underwent profound changes. As has been mentioned above, the Six Day War released a wave of messianic nationalism that took over the religious-Zionist wing of the Israeli political spectrum. The vision of Greater Israel derived from several sources, but the young generation of the National Religious Party became its principal carrier. They provided the settlement movement in the West Bank and the Gaza Strip with its hard core and ended the National Religious Party's traditional alliance with the Labor Party. In 1977, forty years of Labor hegemony in pre-state and Israeli politics ended when Menachem Begin won (or rather the Labor Party lost) the elections of May 1977. During the past twenty-two years (1977-1999) the Likud Alignment held power (i.e., the Prime Minister's post) for fifteen years as against the Labor Party's seven. This has been the result of several forces, but at the heart of the Likud's ability to win elections and form coalitions lies the partnership between the traditional nationalist and bourgeois right-wing strands of Zionism, the radical religious Zionists, and the disenchanted Israelis of Middle Eastern, mostly of North African extraction.[14]

Israel's drive to settle and reclaim the West Bank as a completion of the mission that had not been consummated in 1948 began soon after 1967 and met with halfhearted opposition or meek endorsement by the Labor governments of the day. But after 1977, it was championed much of the time by the Likud governments as the implementation of true Zionism. This turned the West Bank into the single most important arena of the Israeli-Palestinian conflict.

The wedge driven between the Palestinians and the Arab states by the "land for peace" agreements (beginning with the Israeli-Egyptian peace in 1978/1979) only served to exacerbate the Israeli-Palestinian conflict. The same Israeli Prime Minister who was able to reverse some of his own policies and make peace with Egypt launched war in Lebanon in 1982, when he understood that he had obtained a separate peace with Egypt but that his war with the PLO over the West Bank had actually been intensified.

Another negative development during this period was the new significance given to the religious dimension of a conflict that had originally been essentially nationalist and political. Several forces at work converged to bring this about. On the Israeli side, it was the role undertaken by the religious Zionist youth as the vanguard of a second, messianic phase of the Zionist revolution. On the Arab side, the defeat of 1967 contributed to the "return of Islam," to the assumption of a far greater role in public and political life by Islamic movements. This trend reached its zenith in Iran in 1979, when the Islamic revolution toppled the Shah's regime and replaced it with an Islamic Republic. The impact on Arab-Israeli relations was profoundly negative. For some twenty years, Iran had been a tacit but well-known ally of Israel, thereby indicating that a major Muslim country could have a close relationship with Israel at the height of the Arab-Israeli conflict. This was reversed by the Ayatollahs, who undertook to lead a campaign against Israel on religious grounds at the very time that the leading Arab state was making peace with the Jewish state.

Islamic Iran served also as the sponsor of the radical Shiites in Lebanon, who endowed their campaign against Israel's presence in Lebanon with a distinct religious content. A direct link can be drawn from the activities of Hizballah in Lebanon in the early 1980s to the role played in the leadership of Palestinian opposition to Israel and to peace-making with Israel by such Islamic groups as Hamas and Islamic Jihad.[15]

Needless to say, the signing of Israel's peace treaty with Egypt in 1979 was a very positive milestone in the evolution of Israel's relations with the Arab world. But the impact of Israel's new relationship with Egypt on its larger relationship with the Arab world was in fact quite complex. On the positive side of the equation were two cardinal facts: The new relationship had survived several crises and within a decade was accepted by the Arab world as a legitimate fact of life. When Habib Bourghiba, the president of Tunisia, in 1966 raised the idea of recognizing Israel's existence as a more sophisticated measure of confrontation, he was denounced as a traitor. Reactions were mitigated by distance. When Anwar al-Sadat journeyed to Jerusalem and signed the Camp David Accords, the reactions were more bitter and intense. A campaign was led by Syria and Iraq to isolate Egypt, destroy Egyptian-Israeli peace, and bring down the regime that signed it. Sadat was assassinated in 1981, but the regime and peace with Israel survived. Egypt was gradually brought back into the Arab fold, and by the end of the 1980s, Syria restored diplomatic relations with Egypt and, contrary to Asad's vow in 1978, sent an ambassador to Cairo—an Arab capital hosting an Israeli embassy.

The practical and symbolic significance of these developments can hardly be overstated. But their impact was blunted by the emergence of the notion of "cold peace." This was not planned by Sadat in his original strategy but was a policy that he and his successors stumbled upon as their relationship with Israel was taking shape. Cold peace meant Egyptian compliance with the principal stipulations of the peace treaty with Israel—establishing and maintaining diplomatic relations, the implementation and maintenance of the security regime in the Sinai, and of several elements of a normal relationship between two neighboring countries: Egypt is open to Israeli visitors and tourists, postal and telephone links function, and Egypt has allowed a limited economic relationship to develop. But the Egyptian government has prevented or severely limited the development of any other relations—travel by Egyptians to Israel, trade, cultural ties, and the like.

These governmental policies have been reinforced by genuine opposition to Israel and to peace with Israel by various political factions and professional groups—Islamists, neo-Nasserites, and the intelligentsia in general. It is often difficult to separate cause from effect: Government policies have to some extent been a response to authentic opposition, but that opposition has also been nourished by a sense that it was desirable to the government. As a result, a relationship has evolved that is limited and beleaguered. Israel is attacked viciously in the Egyptian media, and economic and intellectual constituencies supportive of peace with Israel have failed to develop.

The strategy of cold peace developed in response to the

failure to implement the Palestinian dimension of the Israeli-Egyptian peace agreement and as an effort to mollify domestic and Arab opposition to Egypt's peace with Israel. In that regard it has been quite successful. But there are additional layers to the concept and practice of cold peace. There is a genuine sense of rivalry and competition between Egypt and Israel. Egypt seeks a leading hegemonic role in the Middle East and regards Israel as an obstacle and as a competitor. Many in Egypt fear Israeli economic or intellectual takeover and regard the limitations imposed by cold peace as an effective defense mechanism.

This policy has had two principal negative effects on the general course of Arab-Israeli relations. On the Arab side, it has served to delay the need to come to grips with Israel as such. If the dangers and price of war could be averted by formal peace, why not avoid the agency of genuine reconciliation with Israel by holding on to cold peace or by developing later the distinction between peace and normalization? In that fashion, Israel as a Jewish-Zionist state could be further seen as an illegitimate entity, and a peaceful relationship with it could be justified as a necessary evil.

On the Israeli side, this policy has played into the hands of those who argue that genuine peace with the Arab world is not feasible. But it has also had a more subtle and perhaps a more significant effect by removing the need to contemplate the ramifications of reconciliation with the Arab world. In the late 1950s, when peace with the Arab world seemed impossible, David Ben Gurion developed the "alliance with the periphery"—a strategic relationship with three non-Arab, pro-Western countries: Turkey, Iran, and Ethiopia. If Israel could not become part of its immediate environment, let it leapfrog over the wall of hostility and build a relationship with the region's external perimeter. That relationship had evaporated by the 1970s, but the prospect of full peace with the principal Arab state raised other possibilities. Could Israel come to terms with its immediate environment? At what cost and under what terms? And if these issues were resolved, could Israel cope with normalcy and open borders? Was it ready for open conduct with its Arab neighbors? Was Israeli society sufficiently coherent to interact with millions of Arabs? Was Israel interested in being part of the region in the cultural sense? Could the Israeli political system survive the end of the siege?

The early Israeli-Egyptian peace process generated some speculative discussion of such issues in the Israeli discourse, but as the euphoria dissipated and the reality of the cold peace crystallized, that discussion came to an end.

The peace process of the 1970s and 1980s was accompanied by a curious discordant note—the UN General Assembly's resolution of November 1975, which denounced Zionism as a form of racism. The resolution was rescinded 16 years later in a move led by the United States. The 1975 resolution and the failure of a single Arab state to support its removal in the immediate aftermath of the Madrid Conference can, of course, be seen as evidence of the Arab world's profound original and lingering opposition to Israel's ideological foundations. But it is as significant to note that the Arab world did not play the principal role in either the introduction or rescission of the UN's resolution. The 1975 vote, it was shown at the time, was in fact a Soviet initiative, while the 1991 measure was openly taken and led by the United States. It was, of course, closely connected to the inauguration of the Madrid process, but the UN's second vote was more a reflection of the Cold War's end than a new Arab approach to Zionism.

1993 to the Present

The Oslo and Washington Accords of August to September, 1993, represented the third turning point in the evolution of Israel's relationship with the Arab world. The Six Day War in June 1967 laid the ground for treating the deadlock of the 1949 to 1967 period and for reaching an Arab-Israeli compromise; the Camp David Accords of September 1978 led to the first full-fledged peace between Israel and a major Arab state and outlined the principles for a resolution of the Palestinian problem (acceptable to that state but not to Palestinian nationalism). In 1993, an agreement was made between Israel and the authoritative representatives of Palestinian nationalism that provided for mutual recognition between Israel and the PLO and established the framework for Palestinian self-rule and for a final status agreement between the two protagonists.

This breakthrough was to some extent a by-product of the great changes that had affected the world and the region during the preceding years—the end of the Cold War, the breakup of the Soviet Union, the Gulf crisis, and the Gulf war—but it was also the product of important developments in Israel and in the Arab world.

In the Arab world at large, the trend toward disengaging from the conflict with Israel that had affected Egypt in the 1970s came to affect others—Saudis, Moroccans, and, in a different manner, Syrians. They did not become enamored of Israel and were not ready to accept Zionism as such, but they were willing to offer Israel formal peace and acceptance in the region in order to deal with more urgent priorities. Among the Palestinians, the grudging acceptance of a two-state solution in 1988 was further developed into acceptance of a junior status in the Madrid peace process and subsequently of the Oslo terms. Yasser Arafat and his associates, headquartered in Tunis and weakened by their support for Saddam Hussein, were willing to settle, at least temporarily, on inferior terms, as long as the principal aim of Palestinian nationalism—statehood—was obscured or precluded.

In Israel, the major change was produced by the June 1992 elections that brought Yitzhak Rabin and the Labor Party to power. Yitzhak Shamir had been firm in his conviction that Israel should hold on to the West Bank, the Gaza Strip, and the Golan Heights. From his vantage point, the changes that had occurred in the world and in the region served both to vindicate and to reinforce Israel's position. Rabin's view was quite different. The circumstances obtaining in the early 1990s provided Israel with an opportunity to come to terms with the Arab world. "Peace for peace" was an empty slogan; to come to a real settlement, concessions would have to be made. Israel's right to the West Bank was as valid as the Arabs', but realistically, Israel could not hold on to the whole West Bank and certainly not to the Gaza Strip. By trying to hold on to the West Bank, Israel was twisting its order of priorities. Resources that should have been invested in Israel proper, in absorbing the Russian immigration and in preparing the country for the next century, were being diverted to the settlements. The real threats to Israel's national security came from Iran and Iraq. Israel had to come to terms with its immediate neighbors in order to deal with the greater threats looming in the East. After fifty years of war and conflict, it was time to take risks in order to use the window of opportunity and set the country on a course of peace.

Rabin did not delude himself into believing that full

peace could be achieved in short order. The road to a comprehensive Arab-Israeli settlement was long and arduous; and
even if such a settlement were to be accomplished, the Middle
East would not turn into a placid, stable place. But Israel must
mount the track leading to a settlement. It could start the
process with an Arab state, Syria, or it could start it with the
Palestinians. After about a year of diplomatic groping and vac-
illation, the die was cast; the first agreement was made with the
PLO in Oslo. Two years later, the Oslo II agreement was
signed in Washington. It too did not address the final status
issues but was much clearer in indicating the Israeli government's willingness to relinquish control of most of the West
Bank and to envisage a Palestinian entity, in all likelihood a
state, in that territory.[16]

The Oslo accords provided the basis for the progress
made in the years 1993 to 1996 in Israeli-Arab normalization—a second full-fledged peace agreement, semi-diplomatic
relations with four additional Arab states, and Israeli participation in three Middle Eastern economic conferences and other
regional forums. As we know, sufficient momentum was not
generated to overcome the difficulties that were built into the
Oslo process, and Oslo accords and the opposition in Israel
and in the Arab world, and the process was suspended in
1996.

It is significant that the cutting edge of the opposition to
a settlement based in compromise on both sides was religious.
On the Israeli side, Rabin's assassin and the perpetrator of the
massacre in the Tomb of the Patriarchs were Orthodox Jews,
members of the hard core of the nationalist religious opposition to the Rabin government and its policies. But in the final
analysis, the Israeli voters' decision in the referendum on Oslo
that was conducted through the May 1996 elections was

grounded in political issues and colored by the loss of personal security. On the Arab side, Hamas, the Islamic Jihad, and Hizballah, which conducted the violent assault in the peace process, are religious movements tied in some fashion to Iran, but the principal decisions affecting the course of the peace process were made in Gaza, Damascus, and Cairo by political leaders.

On the Israeli-Zionist side of the equation, an interesting development occurred when Orthodox Jews and movements abroad (in the US, France, and Australia, to name three communities) challenged the Israeli government's authority to make concessions with regard to the Land of Israel, and more specifically with regard to Jerusalem. From this novel perspective, the government of Israel was no longer seen as a sovereign, unchallenged decision-maker. The Land of Israel and Jerusalem were seen as the sacred property of the Jewish people, temporarily managed by the government of Israel. A Jew did not have to be a Zionist in the classic sense of the term to oppose and seek to obstruct any plan by the government of Israel to cede away parts of the Land of Israel.

The initial successes of the post-1993 peace process generated a fresh discussion of Israel's place in a peaceful Middle East. The dialogue failed even before the onset of the 1996 crisis. The boldest vision on the Israeli side was painted by Shimon Peres as Foreign Minister and in his book *The New Middle East*.[17] In his view, political peace was a necessary prelude to a joint effort by Israelis and Arabs to overcome scarcity of resources, poverty, and overpopulation—the underlying problems that threatened to make the region unlivable in the coming decades.

In Israel, Peres encountered the obvious criticism from the opponents of his policies and skepticism by more conservative peacemakers like Rabin, but in the Arab world, his vision nourished the debate on peace and normalization. The original Egyptian distinction between a warm peace and a cold peace with Israel was not replaced by a distinction between peace and normalization. Peace would be a formal relationship that would end belligerency and give Israel the recognition and the paraphernalia of diplomatic and certain other relations that it so craved. But normalization—cultural, economic and social relations and full acceptance—would be denied. This would protect the Arab world from Israeli domination but would also enable it to keep legitimacy and full acceptance for Israel in abeyance.

The most significant manifestations of resistance to Israel's integration in the region and of the tendency to keep the conflict open-ended were found in Egypt. With the signing of the Oslo Accords, the policy of cold peace could finally be abandoned—but it was not. In 1994/1995, Egypt sought to slow down the normalization with Israel under the banner of opposition to Israel's nuclear potential. But Israelis suspected that while Egypt was genuinely troubled by Israel's nuclear capacity and its strategic manifestiation, Egypt was also using the issue as a convenient mechanism for denying Israel's full accommodation with its Arab neighbors. This was seen as a policy of "shifting the goal post"—always finding a fresh issue to keep the conflict with Israel open-ended.

The Current Agenda

The present perspective on Israel's relationship with the Arab world is colored by diplomatic stalemate and intellectual confusion. The momentum of the years 1993 to 1996 has been checked, and even if an agreement is reached on a second further redeployment, it is difficult to envisage the present Israeli government and Palestinian leadership making any real progress in a negotiation on final status issues. Furthermore, on both sides, every shade of opinion can be heard. It is easy to encounter negative or pessimistic opinions and to reach the conclusion that the prospect of compromise in the early- and mid-1990s was an illusion, and that Israelis and Arabs are condemned to remain locked in conflict.

One does not have to go to the margins to pick up radical discourse. Not long ago, the Israeli public was treated to a long interview with the Prime Minister's father, an 88-year-old eminent historian of medieval Jewish Spain, and a veteran activist of Revisionist Zionism. With great clarity and conviction, he argued in the spirit of the 1920s that there was no hope for an accommodation with the Arab and Muslim worlds, that Israel and the Jewish people must look after themselves, and that the key to survival lay in the Jewish people's strength and coherence. Concessions to the Arabs, he said, would be pointless and dangerous. These views are echoed in the Prime Minister's book of 1993 and occasionally in his contemporary speeches and statements.[18]

If such views are juxtaposed with Arab denunciations of Zionism, opposition to normalization, or Palestinian insistence on "the right of return" as a component of any final status agreement, the prospects for reconciliation and resolution appear bleak. But statesmanship is not about confronting one negative view with another but about identifying genuine opportunities when they present themselves.

A close look at the events of the past five years, the successes and setbacks of the 1993 to 1996 period, and the stalemate of the past thirty months yields two conclusions. One is that the opportunity created in the early 1990s is still available. The broad lines of a historic compromise between Zionism and Palestinian Arab nationalism are readily visible. The majority of Israelis, including a sizable portion of the right, have accepted the notion of Palestinian statehood in the West Bank and the Gaza Strip. The Palestinian leadership has in fact reconciled itself to the idea that the bulk of the settlements and the settlers will stay in place and that the emerging Palestinian state will not comprise the whole of the West Bank. Very important issues have yet to be negotiated, but from the perspective of a century of conflict, the obstacles on the path to a settlement seem eminently surmountable.

The other conclusion is that the finality and clarity that are so important to the Israeli and Jewish side will be difficult to achieve. For one thing, it is difficult to envisage a comprehensive solution that would address the Palestinian and Syrian-Lebanese issues simultaneously. It is also difficult to envisage an Israeli-Palestinian agreement resolving the final status issues in a manner that would facilitate Israel's insistence on full acceptance. To put it in the terms of this conference, the representatives of Palestinian nationalism, and for that matter, other Arab interlocutors are not likely any time soon to endorse the legitimacy of Zionism, even when they come to terms with the reality of Israel. The distinction between peace and normalization is likely to be maintained as one of the principal instruments for demonstrating that items of unfinished business have remained on the Arab-Israeli agenda.

This very tendency militates against a genuine Israeli and Jewish sense of insecurity. Some wonder about the value of a political settlement that rests on one party's lingering refusal to accept the other party's legitimacy. Others worry about a tendency to keep the conflict open-ended. If such issues as Jerusalem, the Palestinian refugees, and Arab opposition to Israel's nuclear potential remain open and could be galvanized at any point in the future, how stable can a solution be? And how wise would it be for Israel to concede territory for the sake of less than a final and definite resolution?

The answer to these questions lies in an incremental strategy. If a satisfactory, comprehensive settlement is not readily available, it does not follow that Israel should dig in and adopt policies likely to undermine the prospect of a future accommodation. Israel's reconciliation with the Arab world should be seen as a process to be implemented over time.

In years past, various Arab representatives and spokesmen argued that for Israel to be fully acceptable to the Arab world, it would have to change its character and become a part of the region. This demand was never put in precise terms but was articulated through opposition to Israel's "Western" or "pro-Western" orientation and to Zionist ideology. The notion that Israel was not a nation-state or a territorially defined political community but the national home of a people spread around the globe. These motifs still appear in anti-Israeli and anti-Jewish books and articles in the Arab world, but the demand as such has not been raised in any recent serious give-and-take between Israel and its Arab interlocutors.

The only Arab spokesmen who raise a serious demand that Israel de-Zionize or transform itself in some other fashion are some of the most prominent intellectuals and politicians who speak for about a million Palestinians known as Israel's "Arab minority" or "Israeli Arabs." This terminology is no longer acceptable to members of a group who prefer to refer to themselves as Palestinians who are Israeli citizens. They now constitute between 16 and 20 percent of Israel's population (depending on whether the population of East Jerusalem is taken into account), and their electoral and political weight is likely to increase in a political system in which elections are determined by the shifting of 2 or 3 percent of the voters across the political system's median line.

Although they now refer to themselves as Palestinians, the members of Israel's Arab minority do not wish to join a prospective Palestinian state. They view themselves as Israeli citizens who seek to change or transform Israel's body politic. Be they comparative moderates who want a larger share of the public pie or cultural autonomy, or radicals who want a non-Zionist Israel or a binational state, Israel's present character as the national state of the Jewish people with a significant national minority is not acceptable to them. The preoccupation of most Israeli Arabs with mundane matters rather than with the underlying issues of principle and the fragmented politics of their community have thus far mitigated the issue, but it is certain to acquire greater import and urgency in the coming years.

Curiously, while the major participants in Israel's public and political discourse split hairs in discussing the pros and cons of Palestinian statehood and other solutions and approaches to the Israeli-Palestinian conflict, little attention is paid to the awkward relationship between the Israeli state and nearly a fifth of its population, except by a small group of experts and election specialists. The one part of the current Israeli discourse that is affected by the issue is the post-Zionist debate, in which Israeli Arab intellectuals have added their voices to the demand to redefine Israel's political community on a new, non-Zionist basis.

It would be useful in this context to quote several passages from a recent interview given by Azmi Bishara, the most eloquent Israeli Arab politician and intellectual and currently a Member of Knesset.[19]

> I do not rule out a temporary solution of two states for two peoples, but this cannot be more than a temporary solution...ultimately the framework must be binational...

> A distinction must be made between a historic compromise and a settlement. A settlement can be made without a historic compromise, but it would be limited in its time range and would lack the moral and historic dimensions...[The Zionist left] speaks about the '67 problem as if the '48 problem did not exist...if you ask me whether a Zionist peace is possible I would say that a settlement, maybe even a comparatively just settlement, is possible but not a final, comprehensive peace, the end of the conflict. In such an event the struggle against Zionism will continue in other forms. It could possibly turn from a national to a civic struggle. In that case our role as Arab citizens of Israel could become the most important...

> If we speak of the national conflict the solution is the decolonization of the occupied territories in the West Bank and Gaza. But if we speak of the civic problem the solution is Israel's dezionization.

Azmi Bishara is a participant in a debate that deals with both current politics and past events. Like the other participants in this debate, he has a narrative of the previous century and a prescription for the present and the future. The narrative and the prescription are mutually reinforcing and contribute to the context within which the history of Zionism's relationship with the Arab world is seen and written. This is true of every history but is particularly significant for an unfolding conflict in which context and perspective keep changing.

During the past decade or so, the historiography of Zionism's and Israel's relationship with the Arab world has been altered in several significant ways. For one thing, archives have been opened and invaluable sources have been made available for crucial periods and turning points. The progress of the peace process and the signing of three major Arab-Israeli agreements since 1977 tend to reinforce the argument that peace and accommodation could have reached much earlier.

The formation of Israel's first right-wing government in 1977 and the right wing's ascendancy during the last twenty-two years have had a different, powerful impact on the current view of the earlier phases of Israel's history and its relationship with the Arab world. In 1976, after more than four decades of Labor hegemony, it could be seen and portrayed as mainstream, while Revisionist Zionism could be seen explicitly or implicitly as peripheral. In 1980, one could argue that Begin's victory in 1977 was accidental and his government a passing phenomenon. This is no longer argued in 1999, and contemporary scholarship tends correctly to take a fresh look at the Revisionist movement and other right-wing groups in the 1920s, 1930s, and 1940s and their lingering impact. The power of the state is also brought to bear and serves to change the view of what is central and what is peripheral in Zionist and Israeli history. A right-wing school of historical revisionism is assailing the traditional centrist version of Zionist and Israeli historiography that has been attacked by the left-wing revisionism of the "new historians."[20]

Israel is not faced with a single dilemma and with one choice. In the coming years, it will have to make several fundamental decisions about its own character and related decisions about its relationship with its Arab environment. The choice Israel is presently called to make concerns its relationship with Zionism's historic adversary—Palestinian nationalism.

As we have seen, the avoidable compromise is more attractive than the options that may have been available at various points in the past. The proposed compromise is quite attractive but lacks the finality that Israelis crave and, needless to say, entails concessions that many Israelis abhor. This author, for one, thinks Israel should take it.

Notes

1. Najib Azoury, *Le Reveil de la Nation Arabe* (Paris, 1905), p. V.

2. On Azoury's political activity see: Martin Kramer, "Azoury: A Further Episode," *Middle Eastern Studies*, Vol. 18 No. 4 (October, 1982), pp. 351-358; Elie Kedourie, *Arabic Political Memoirs and Other Studies* (London, 1974), pp. 107-123; Stefan Wild, "Negib Azoury and his book *Le Reveil de la Nation Arabe"* in Marwan R. Buheiry (ed.), *Intellectual Life in the Arab East 1890-1939* (Beirut, 1981), pp. 92-104.

3. Yosef Gorny, *Zionism and the Arabs 1882-1948* (Oxford, 1987), pp. 11-77.

4. Neville J. Mandel, *The Arabs and Zionism before World War I* (Berkeley, 1976); Unpublished M.A thesis by Ya'acov Ro'i, "Yahas Ha-Yishuv el Ha-aravim: 1880-1914" [The attitude of the "Yishuv" to the Arabs, in Hebrew] (Jerusalem, 1964); Walter Laqueur, *A History of Zionism* (New York, 1972).

5. Yehoshua Porat, *The Emergence of the Palestinian-Arab National Movement* (London, 1974).

6. J.C. Hurewitz, *The Struggle for Palestine* (New York, 1950).

7. Shlomo Avineri, *The Making of Modern Zionism* (New York, 1981); Sasson Sofer, *Zionism and the Foundation of Israeli Diplomacy* (Cambridge, 1998).

8. Shabtai Teveth, *Ben Gurion and the Palestinian Arabs* (Oxford, 1985).

9. Yehoshua Porat, *Bemivkhan Hama'ase Hapolity* [Tested by Political Action, in Hebrew] (Jerusalem, 1985), pp. 65-119, 323-330.

10. For a classic statement of the Arab nationalist grievance and view of Zionism see: Albert Hourani, *Syria and Lebanon, A Political Essay* (London, 1946).

11. Itamar Rabinovich, *The Road Not Taken* (New York, 1991).

12. The term was coined by Nadav Safran, *From War to War* (New York, 1969), pp. 42-47.

13. Malcolm Kerr, *The Arab Cold War* (London, 1971).

14. The transformation of Israeli politics during the last three decades is very well described in: Daniel Ben Simon, *Eretz Aheret* [Another Country, in Hebrew] (Tel Aviv, 1997). For an earlier penetrating description and analysis see: Amos Oz, *In the Land of Israel* (London, 1983).

15. Fouad Ajami, *The Arab Predicament* (Cambridge, England, 1982) and Fouad Ajami, *The Dream Palace of the Arabs* (New York, 1998).

16. Itamar Rabinovich, *The Brink of Peace* (Princeton, 1998).

17. Shimon Peres, *The New Middle East* (New York, 1993).

18. For this interview see: *Ha'aretz*, September 18, 1998. See also Benjamin Netanyahu, *A Place Among the Nations* (New York, 1993) and Netanyahu's speech in the Israeli National Security college: *IDF Radio*, August 14, 1997.

19. See an interview with Dr. Azmi Bishara in: *Ha'aretz*, May 29, 1998.

20. For examples of right-wing revisionism, see the publications of the Ariel Center based in the West Bank and the journal *Nativ*. For the controversy with the New Historians, see: Efraim Karsh, *Fabricating History: The New Historians* (London, 1997). Karsh addresses in his book, among others: Avi Shlaim, *The Politics of Partition: King Abdullah, The Zionists and Palestine, 1951-1971* (Oxford, 1990); Ilan Pappe, *The Making of the Arab-Israeli Conflict 1947-1951* (New York, 1988); Benny Morris, *1948 and After* (Oxford, 1994)

THE ZIONIST LEGACY
AND THE FUTURE OF ISRAEL

Shlomo Avineri

Israel is a credal, goal-oriented society, established to realize an ideological telos. It also constantly judges itself by its goals, and it is this tension between ideology and reality which endows Israeli public life, for better or for worse, with much of its drive as well as its constant self-criticism, back-biting, and internal bickering.

One way of looking at the degree to which Israel has lived up to the criteria set up by its dreamers and founders or failed to do so is to look at some of the foundational writings that inspired the Zionist movement. Such a confrontation between utopian vision and historical reality may also serve as a road map for Israel's future.

Many texts could be chosen, yet it would not be too arbitrary to choose two of Theodor Herzl's major publications as benchmarks by which to judge Israel's reality against the dream: his programmatic *The Jewish State* (1896) and his utopian novel *Altneuland* (1902).

Out of Herzl's multifaceted projections as to what the Jewish commonwealth should be that are embedded in these two works, the following appear to be salient to our discourse (of course, others could also be chosen).

1) The Jewish state, having been established through diplomacy and a universal *consensus gentium*, will not have any enemies. It will be neutral and will need only a rudimentary

military force for the most basic functions of preserving public order and security.

2) While religion in the Jewish state will be revered and respected as part of the national heritage ("We are a nation through our religion," Herzl wrote in his diaries), rabbis' authority will be limited to the confines of the synagogue, just like the army should be confined to its barracks. No clerical interference in politics should be tolerated, though the Sabbath and Jewish holidays will be publicly respected as days of rest.

3) The Jewish commonwealth will be a multilingual (today one would say multicultural) society, "like Switzerland": Each Jewish community immigrating to Palestine will keep the linguistic and cultural traditions of its country of origin; German theater and French opera will flourish side by side. Hebrew could not and should not be the language of the land: It is, according to Herzl, a totally defunct, merely sacral language ("Who among us may even buy a train ticket in Hebrew?"), and its introduction as the country's sole language would cut it off from world culture and establish another parochial "neo-Hebraic" mini-nation comparable to modern Greece. Only by keeping various European tongues as the modes of intercourse and communication in the Jewish land will the country continue to maintain its links with cultural and intellectual trends prevalent in the wider European world.

4) Herzl never envisaged a conflict with the Arab world or with a national movement of Palestinian Arabs, although he was aware of the existence of an Arab population in Palestine (one of the heroes of *Altneuland* is a cultured, European-educated Arab engineer from Haifa who welcomes the Jewish immigration in the name of progress and modernization and is elected as one of the leaders of the New Society). One

should add that in Herzl's time, there existed no Arab national movement to speak of, neither in Palestine nor in the neighboring Arab countries, though in his diaries Herzl comments on the British illusion of being able to hold on to Egypt in the face of the emergence of an Egyptian intellectual elite, Western-educated and European-oriented, which he identifies as "the masters of tomorrow." Yet in the Palestinian context, he viewed the Arab population in terms of merely formal, legal, individual equality, coupled with cultural respect for their tradition. The Arab residents of the Jewish New Society in Palestine would be equal citizens; *Altneuland* has as one of its main subplots a futile attempt of a Jewish racist political movement to try to deprive the Arab citizens of the Jewish commonwealth of their equal rights, and fails dismally in the elections.

On all of these points Herzl was wrong, in the sense that the developments went in another direction. If there is one common thread to Herzl's miscalculations, it is his inadequate consideration of Jewish realities, mainly in the Eastern European context, as well as his inability to foresee correctly developments in the Middle East. Perhaps on the last count he should not be faulted, as he was a child of his time, when liberalism did not yet envisage the end of European hegemony and the emergence of national movements in the non-European world. Yet the fact remains that for all of his liberalism and universalism, black spots remained in Herzl's vision of the regional context of the emergence of a Jewish commonwealth in the Middle East.

Yet it would be a mistake to dismiss Herzl's vision as a mere chimera. His vision was nurtured by the liberal, tolerant traditions of Europe at the fin de siècle, and it was these traditions that he saw unravelling with the emergence of populist, nationalistic, and intolerant movements, which to his mind threatened the fragile texture of the multiethnic, tolerant Austro-Hungarian Empire. These developments gave rise in his own Vienna to the emergence of such radical populists as Lueger and such radical racists as von Schonerer. Their appearance and the crumbling of the liberal, tolerant order of the Hapsburg monarchy meant to him that Jews would be caught in the crossfire. Herzl's vision in Altneuland is a noble, perhaps even slightly pathetic attempt to rebuild a liberal Vienna on the shores of the eastern Mediterranean.

Yet beyond these historical contexts, there is a further aspect that makes Herzl's predictions, though largely falsified by subsequent historical developments, relevant to the current public discourse in Israel: They all point to what (to my mind) are the crucial open questions of the Zionist project—as well as to its open wounds. As such, they may serve as a compass to the trajectory to be taken by the Jewish state in the future. In other words, these open questions are a key to whether Israel will, in the future, be able to be at peace with its surrounding environment as well as with itself—and with the vision that created it.

Because the achievements of Zionism and Israel are so astounding and impressive, a mere triumphalist reiteration of them in a celebratory mood is superfluous, and—because of its self-congratulatory nature—also tends to be smug and occasionally arrogant and unfeeling. A critical look at what are still open questions may be a much more fruitful approach.

The major and most crucial goal for Israel is to arrive at a situation in which it lives in peace with its neighbors. This is a difficult and tortuous path, and pious reiterations of the need for peace will not suffice. The major premise, however, without which no chance for even a minimal reconciliation is possible, has been the Zionist movement's acceptance, after much soul-searching, of the principle of partition of the historical Land of Israel—the idea of two states for two nations. It was this acceptance of partition in 1947 that made the establishment of the State of Israel possible, internationally acceptable, and morally legitimate. The Six Day War now appears, in retrospect, as a reversal of this acceptance on the part of many Israelis, and the emergence of a messianic linkage between radical nationalism and religion is one of the heavy prices Israel is now paying for the victory of 1967. In this sense, undoing one of the consequences of 1967 is the major challenge for a moderate compromise-oriented Zionism, bringing Zionism back, so to speak, not only to its liberal origins but also to its senses. Is this possible? Is the internal structure of Israel, with the messianisation of large sectors of religious (and even non-religious) Zionism, capable of this? This is an unresolved question: The Oslo accords are an important milestone in this direction; the much more assertive policies of the Netanyahu government, which came to power in the wake of the assassination of Prime Minister Yitzhak Rabin, give rise to serious questions in this regard; the tribulations of the Wye River Memorandum give mixed signals of both hope and skepticism. But let it be said clearly and unequivocally: Without the acceptance of partition, no peace is possible. This does not mean that the other side is unambiguously ready for compromise. Nonetheless, the acceptance of partition is a condition *sine qua non* for any future peace settlement.

The paradox is that the more secure Israel is—and with the demise of the Soviet Union as a strategic umbrella for radical Arab nationalism, Israel is today more strategically secure than at any time since its establishment—the more internal, divisive issues will come to the fore and present new challenges to Israel's society and culture. Many view this as a threat to the cohesion or even survivability of Israel as a nation, but that is not necessarily the case. The revolutionary ingredient, immanent in the Zionist project, is a redefinition of Jewish identity in a post-Enlightenment world. Nurtured by the ideas of the Enlightenment, Zionism inherited also the burden of its dialectics: Having both liberalism and nationalism as its pillars, Zionism and Israel embody all the contradictions of the modern nation-state—how to achieve self-determination as well as how to transcend nationalistic particularism within a universalistic framework.

Will Israel be capable of developing a Jewish identity and Hebrew culture in touch with both the historical roots of an ever-changing Jewish tradition and the new trends of world culture? Can a middle way be found between an abstract, theoretical secularism, sometimes devoid of context and specificity, and a militant nationalism? Or will Israeli society be hijacked by a retrograde, ethnocentric, exclusivist, even racist construction of Jewishness that is, in a most fundamental way, exilic, based on a self-righteous perception of Jews in the Galuth, immersed in their perceptions of their own victimization and thus oblivious to the claims of the Other and to universalistic values?

This leads directly to the dilemma of how to deal with power, both political and military: a novelty in Jewish history. The perennial philosophical question of the ethics of power could justifiably have been overlooked and disregarded in the Diaspora and substituted by the ethics of powerlessness that made Jewish thought and behavior so morally appealing. Yet even thinkers like Yehuda Halevi, in his *Sefer ha-Kuzari*, were aware that the issue may come back to haunt Jews once they regained political power. The issue has constantly accompanied the Zionist movement and was at the core of the dispute between liberal and Labour Zionism on one hand and Revisionism on the other. Eventually, as Anita Shapira has shown in her studies, a legitimization of a controlled use of power was adopted, with a heavy heart, by mainstream Zionism, and it has largely imbued the ethics of the Israeli Army. For all their excesses during the Intifada, the Israel Defense Forces behaved less savagely than other armies of democratic countries behaved in analogous situations (France and Britain come easily to mind). Yet the memory of the Holocaust and the helplessness implied by it has sometimes been used by many Israelis and Diaspora Jews to justify, under the mantle of victimhood, unconscionable behavior. For all its vulnerability, Israel has to come to terms with its preponderant strength, with the fact that when Israel is bombing Beirut it is not the Israelis who are the helpless victims of a Warsaw Ghetto–like situation.

It is especially riling that such a confrontation with the dilemma of the ethics of power has failed to engage, with some notable exceptions, the kind of soul-searching one would expect within religious circles in Israel—especially the established Rabbinate, many of whose members appear to have come down on the side of a rather unreflective triumphalist idolization of power.

The exigencies of war and siege have also made it difficult to deal adequately with many of the issues connected with the immanent tensions between the institutional structures of the nation-state and democratic principles. All democracies suffer from the need to confront these challenges, and not all of them have come up with satisfactory answers, as numerous recent examples from France, Britain, and Germany, as well as the United States would easily suggest. Yet the continuous war situation provided a convenient alibi—in many cases, not even to admit that a problem existed and to subsume the complex dilemmas involving the Arab minority in Israel (I am not referring here to the occupied territories) under the rubric of "security." For all the formal, legal equality and participation in elections enjoyed by the Arab citizens of Israel, too many aspects of unjustified and unjustifiable discrimination against them were legitimized, even by many liberal Israeli Jews, by referring to security considerations; and while, by and large, Israel treated its Arab citizens better than many other democracies under conditions of war and emergency (the American treatment of citizens of Japanese origin during World War II comes to mind), the time has come for Israel to do away with a whole web of legislation and practice that discriminate against Arabs in matters of land use, job opportunities, housing, school funding, and so on.

Having said that, it should be pointed out that on the symbolic level, the construction of Israel as a Jewish nation-state will—and should—be preserved, and some clear distinction has to be made between the need to abolish any form of discrimination and the symbolic level. It is not an easy distinction, yet it has to be made.

One can well understand the difficulty of an Israeli Arab citizen in identifying with the sentiments expressed in "Hatikva," the Israeli national anthem, which is based on a Jewish discourse and a Jewish hope for a return to Zion. Yet one should equally understand the difficulties of a British secular Jew who may be a republican in identifying with "God Save the Queen" (especially when the sovereign also happens to be the head of the Established Church of England). One can well understand the unease of an Israeli Arab in identifying with the Star of David or the menorah, with their obvious Jewish connotations. Yet one should equally understand a similar unease of British Orthodox Jews or devout Muslims when they are supposed to swear allegiance to the Union Jack, which is, after all, a double cross (England's St. George's entwined with that of Scotland's St. Andrew)—and the cross appears on the state emblems of numerous other European democracies, from the Scandinavian countries to Greece. Those aspects of the symbolic level are obvious hardships for minorities, and while minorities should not be discriminated against, on the symbolic level minorities are not entitled to deprive majorities of their symbolic points of reference and identification—neither in Britain nor in Israel. This has to be said clearly and loudly, but it has moral force only if Israel does away with the institutional vestiges of discrimination against its Arab citizens.

So as not to leave room for doubt, the Law of Return is part of the symbolic heritage of Israel as a Jewish state—just as a Law of Return would, hopefully, one day be part of the heritage of an independent Palestinian state. As a law of immigration, it is obviously discriminatory: All laws of immigration are, either on the basis of wealth, health, education, the country's preference for persons possessing certain skills, descent, and so on. The Israeli Law of Return—just like a future Palestinian Law of return would be—is a symbol of solidarity, and justified as such.

The fact that Arabic is the second official language of Israel is another example of a context that already exists for what is basically a legally mandated multiculturalism (without being called so). It should be further developed by allocating adequate and equal funds for the Arab language school sector and by leaving curriculum decision-making in the hands of local Arab authorities rather than with bureaucrats in the Ministry of Education who are mostly Jewish. Years of neglect have to be overcome to bring Arab schools to the level of Hebrew schools in Israel, but the very recognition that Israeli Arabs have a right to education in their language and culture is an important building block for further preservation of Arab culture within what is and what will remain a Jewish state.

The cultural autonomy of Israeli Arabs should be institutionally widened and should not be hampered by Jewish fears of irredentism; Israel is strong enough to withstand such pressures. The residue of the Ottoman *millet* system, which leaves matters of family law in the hands of the religious authorities of the respective religious/ethnic communities, should not be seen as a mere retrograde measure buttressing clerical power; it could be equally seen and developed as an ingredient of pluralism and multiculturalism, provided adequate exit strategies were available for those who would like to opt out (civil marriage, for example).

All this, it should be added, will be possible only under conditions of furthering the peace process. Otherwise, Israeli Arabs will continue to be seen as hostages to the conflict.

This brings us to the last two issues I would like to address as challenges that Israel cannot avoid, and both are related to Ahad Ha'am's vision of the moral context of the Jewish state as a "spiritual center." First, there is a need to revive the social vision of Israeli society, which has been greatly diminished along with the dwindling importance of many of its erstwhile unique institutions—a high degree of egalitarianism, the kibbutz movement, the Histadruth. An Israel shorn of this moral content will not become a focus of identification for Jews in the Diaspora and will become more and more irrelevant to them.

Relations with the Diaspora is the second pillar of this Ahad Ha'amic vision of the moral dimension of Israel. For decades, those relations were seen as dominated by an Israeli attitude that viewed Jews in the affluent Diaspora in purely instrumentalist terms—as a resource for political support and economic assistance. With both the lessening of the existential dangers to Israel as well as its own growing economic prosperity, this instrumentalist agenda becomes less and less relevant.

To make Israel into a living, existential reality for the Jews in the Diaspora requires new institutional frameworks, as well as an Israeli willingness to listen to the voices of Jews who do not live nor intend to live in Israel. It will equally require Diaspora Jewry—especially in the United States—to develop new structures of leadership beyond those mandated by the philanthropic nature of most Jewish organizations which makes leadership by major contributors into an almost exclusive norm. Especially in the US, the spiritual and institutional richness of the Jewish community, with tens of thousands of academics, intellectuals, writers, artists, musicians, journalists, and so on, who are at present almost totally absent from community life and leadership structures, has to be tapped. Only then will a true intellectual dialogue with Israel be possible; it cannot be limited, on the US side, to fundraisers, rabbis, and professional community workers. The American Jewish community is much richer than that, just as Israel is much richer than is typically acknowledged by the propagandists sent abroad for fundraising and mobilizing public support.

All this may be a heavy burden for a small and still partially beleaguered nation. But the creativity evidenced by Israel's achievements gives one great hope that the open questions—or open wounds—can be addressed as successfully as the challenges of survival or the momentous gathering in of the exiles. It is a question of moral and political will, and if we will it, it will not be a fable.

CONTRIBUTORS

STEVEN J. ZIPPERSTEIN is the Daniel E. Koshland Professor in Jewish Culture and History at Stanford University, where he is also the Taube Director of the Program in Jewish Studies. He has taught at Oxford, Cornell, UCLA, École des Hautes Études en Sciences Sociales, and at universities in Russia, Poland, and Israel. He is the author of two award-winning books, *The Jews of Odessa: A Cultural History, 1794-1881* (Stanford University Press, 1985), and *Elusive Prophet: Ahad Ha'am and the Origins of Zionism* (University of California Press, 1993). His most recent book is *Imagining Russian Jewry: Memory, History, Identity* (University of Washington Press, 1999). He is an editor of the journal, *Jewish Social Studies: History, Culture, and Society.*

YARON EZRAHI is Professor of Political Science at the Hebrew University of Jerusalem and is a senior fellow at the Israel Democracy Institute, where he heads the program on Mass Communications and the Democratic Process in Israel. Noteworthy among his publications is his book, *The Descent of Icarus: Science and the Transformation of Contemporary Democracy*, published by Harvard University Press in 1990. His most recent book is *Rubber Bullets: Power and Conscience in Modern Israel*, published by Farrar, Straus and Giroux, New York, 1997. This book received the Jewish National Book Award for 1997.

ITAMAR RABINOVICH, the President of Tel Aviv University and Chief Negotiator with Syria and a former Israeli Ambassador to the United States, has held the Yona and Dina Ettinger Chair in the Contemporary History of the Middle East at Tel Aviv University. He was Head of the Shiloah Institute and the Moshe Dayan Center from 1980 to 1989. His research has centered on the modern history of Syria and Lebanon, inter-Arab relations, and Arab-Israeli relations. His most recent publications include the following: *Waging Peace, The Brink of Peace*, and *The Road Not Taken*.

SHLOMO AVINERI is Herbert Samuel Professor of Political Science and Director of the Institute for European Studies at the Hebrew University of Jerusalem. Among his books are: *The Political and Social Thought of Karl Marx, Hegel's Theory of the Modern State, Israel and the Palestinians, The Making of Modern Zionism, Moses Hess: Prophet of Communism and Zionism*, and *Arlosoroff*. He recently wrote an extensive historical introduction to a Hebrew translation of Theodor Herzl's *Diaries*.

Conference Program

Truth from the Land of Israel: Reflections on Zionism's Successes, Failures, and Prospects at 100

Sponsored by the Dorot Foundation in association with The New School for Social Research and YIVO Institute for Jewish Research
October 25-26, 1998

Shlomo Avineri, Department of Political Science, Hebrew University of Jerusalem

Menachem Brinker, Committee for Jewish Studies, University of Chicago; Department of Philosophy, Hebrew University of Jerusalem

Mitchell Cohen, Bernard Baruch College, CUNY

Yaron Ezrahi, Department of Political Science, Hebrew University of Jerusalem

Ernest S. Frerichs, Executive Director, Dorot Foundation

Judith Friedlander, Dean, Graduate Faculty of Political and Social Science, The New School for Social Research

Paula E. Hyman, Program in Judaic Studies, Yale University

Tony Judt, Remarque Institute, New York University

Avishai Margalit, Department of Philosophy, Hebrew University of Jerusalem

Adi Ophir, The Institute for the History and Philosophy of Science and Ideas, Tel Aviv University

Derek Penslar, Department of History, University of Toronto

Itamar Rabinovich, President, Tel Aviv University

Anita Shapira, Department of Jewish History, Tel Aviv University

Fritz Stern, Department of History, Columbia University

Yael Tamir, Department of Philosophy, Tel Aviv University

Michael Walzer, Institute for Advanced Study, Princeton

Leon Wieseltier, Literary Editor, *The New Republic*

Yael Zerubavel, Center for the Study of Jewish Life, Rutgers University

Steven J. Zipperstein, Department of History, Stanford University